Students in the Driver's Seat

Bringing voice, choice, and joy to learning in your classroom

Erin Quinn

Tara Vandertoorn

Pembroke Publishers Limited

© 2025 Pembroke Publishers
538 Hood Road
Markham, Ontario, Canada L3R 3K9
www.pembrokepublishers.com

Library and Archives Canada Cataloguing in Publication

Title: Students in the driver's seat : bringing voice, choice, and joy to learning in your
classroom / Erin Quinn & Tara Vandertoorn.

Names: Quinn, Erin, 1982- author | Vandertoorn, Tara, author.

Description: Includes bibliographical references and index.

Identifiers: Canadiana (print) 20250103095 | Canadiana (ebook) 20250103133 | ISBN
9781551383736 (softcover) | ISBN 9781551389738 (PDF)

Subjects: LCSH: Inquiry-based learning. | LCSH: Student participation in curriculum
planning. | LCSH: Classroom management. | LCSH: Students—Self-rating of. | LCSH:
Teaching.

Classification: LCC LB1027.23 .Q56 2025 | DDC 371.39—dc23

Editor: David Kilgour
Cover Design: John Zehethofer
Typesetting: Jay Tee Graphics Ltd.

Printed and bound in Canada
9 8 7 6 5 4 3 2 1

Contents

Voice and Choice Guide

Each of the strategies listed in this table helps develop one or more dimensions of voice and types of choice as shown. If you are looking to target a specific dimension of voice or type of choice, this table can be used to cross-reference which tools or strategies might be most effective. For more detail about each dimension of voice and type of choice, see Part 1.

Strategy	Dimensions of Voice												Types of Choice			
	Developing and expressing an opinion	Communicating academic concepts	Building a skill	Implementing engagement strategies	Fostering self-awareness	Building commuity	Encouraging independence	Making decisions	Identifying possibilities	Thinking creatively	Collaborating	Encouraging metacognition	Mode/Form	Topic/Resource	Outcome	Time and Sequence
AI for Voice and Choice (p. 34)	✓	✓	✓	✓	✓	✓	✓	✓	✓	✓	✓	✓	✓	✓	✓	✓
Bootcamps (p. 36)			✓		✓					✓	✓			✓	✓	
Checklists (p. 39)			✓	✓			✓					✓				✓
Decision Paralysis Tools (p. 42)								✓		✓			✓	✓		
Flat Sheets (p. 44)		✓	✓				✓			✓	✓					✓
Idea Generators (p. 48)				✓					✓	✓			✓	✓		
Kanban Board (p. 52)							✓	✓			✓		✓			✓
Peer Feedback Frameworks (p. 54)	✓	✓								✓	✓		✓	✓	✓	✓
Plussing (p. 60)						✓			✓	✓	✓		✓	✓		
Time Management Strategies (p. 62)					✓		✓					✓				✓
Skill Builders (p. 65)	✓	✓	✓	✓			✓	✓					✓	✓	✓	✓
Affinity Mapping (p. 75)				✓		✓		✓	✓					✓		
Brainstorming Possibilities (p. 79)		✓		✓					✓	✓	✓			✓		

Category	Attribute	Centres with Choice (p. 83)	Choice Boards (p. 92)	Gamification (p. 95)	Heat Mapping (p. 98)	Inventories (p. 101)	Synthesizing Learner Outcomes (p. 111)	Live Drafts (p. 113)	Whole-Class Activities to Build Transfer Skills (p. 116)	Self-Directed Mini Lessons (p. 119)	Student-Designed Projects (p. 127)	Walk and Talk (p. 130)	Celebration of Learning (p. 136)	Conferenecing (p. 138)	Self-Reflection Tools (p. 141)	Sticky Note Feedback (p. 143)	Student-Led Parent-Teacher Interviews (p. 146)
Types of Choice	Time and Sequence	✓	✓	✓						✓	✓			✓	✓	✓	
	Outcome		✓		✓		✓							✓	✓		
	Topic/Resource		✓		✓	✓			✓	✓	✓	✓	✓	✓	✓	✓	✓
	Mode/Form		✓	✓	✓	✓				✓	✓	✓	✓				✓
Dimensions of Voice	Encouraging metacognition						✓			✓	✓		✓	✓	✓	✓	✓
	Collaborating			✓							✓			✓			
	Thinking creatively			✓							✓						
	Identifying possibilities					✓	✓				✓		✓				✓
	Making decisions		✓	✓	✓	✓		✓			✓	✓	✓				✓
	Encouraging independence	✓		✓		✓				✓	✓		✓	✓			
	Building commuity			✓	✓				✓			✓	✓				✓
	Fostering self-awareness					✓				✓	✓		✓	✓	✓	✓	✓
	Implementing engagement strategies	✓	✓	✓	✓		✓	✓	✓	✓			✓	✓			✓
	Building a skill	✓		✓						✓	✓					✓	
	Communicating academic concepts		✓	✓			✓		✓	✓	✓			✓	✓		
	Developing and expressing an opinion				✓			✓	✓			✓	✓				✓

Preface

This book comes out of a long-term professional and personal relationship between two educators. Here are our individual accounts of how it all began.

Erin

In 2017, I began a journey at a brand-new school and spent my first year there working on my own, trying to figure out how to teach middle-school students to love the Humanities. In my second year, our school was growing and we were in a position to hire an additional teacher for another section of grade 8 language arts and social studies. We were lucky to hire Tara.

Tara and I began our professional relationship very intentionally. We are very different people, but we share a lot of the same values and beliefs about learning. We talked about these values and beliefs often in the early years. Engagement was something we talked about frequently. We wanted to design learning experiences for our students in such a way that they would feel excited and interested in what they were learning and doing. We noticed these conversations always touched on the topics of student voice and choice. If students are to be engaged in their learning, they must have a vested interest in what they are doing. To have a vested interest, they must make choices and have control over what they do and how they do it.

Tara

I returned to my hometown after spending most of my adult career teaching abroad at international schools. When I joined my current school board it was as a substitute teacher — which gave me flexibility with my family as we navigated a massive relocation and enabled me to be a magpie, collecting the best bits from all the classrooms I was a guest in. Eventually, I landed an interview at a beautiful new K–9 school. In the interview were the principal, the assistant principal, and the grade eight learning leader. Little did I know that that thirty-minute interview would become the start of one of the most beautiful collaborative relationships of my career. Erin and I began working together slowly, establishing a foundation of shared pedagogical beliefs about how kids learn best and how to respect and honor diversity in our classrooms. Our road to active collaboration began with a shared moment of acknowledging that we wanted to do better and recognizing that, together, we could do better.

Together

And together we did do better. Collaboration is such a huge part of how we got to the point where we could do something great. As Erin said, we are very different people. There are a lot of things we *don't* have in common. But the thing we do share is a common belief in students. We believe that if we trust in our students, they can and will do great things.

We suspect that if you're picking up this book it is because you believe that your students have something important to share. Our first piece of advice to you is to find someone to read this book with. Find a colleague or friend who shares your belief that students are not "problems" to be solved on the road to success but rather partners in the learning journey. Find a person who would like to talk about this with you, and collaborate and brainstorm ways you might empower your students in your own unique contexts. Find someone who believes that learning shouldn't be something that is "done to students" but something that challenges students to take ownership and master autonomy. This is the essential heart work that accompanies this book and it is easier and much more joyful when you have a partner on the road.

You can find us on Instagram — Erin @msequinn and Tara @mrs.vandertoorn. We post and share our work at www.creativitycollective.ca.

How This Book Works

This book is divided into four parts: "Laying the Foundation," "Building a Toolkit," "Teaching Protocols and Task Design," and "Assessment." You do not have to read the book in order, nor are the tools organized as sequential lessons. Our intention is to provide you with *what* you need *when* you need it, so that you can start incorporating more voice and choice right now. Then you can keep adding more as you see the benefits and value in your classroom.

We have sorted the tools in a variety of ways to show you which ones work well together, but don't let yourself be limited by our ideas. There is more than one right way to do this, so feel free to hack, adapt, and add to all the ideas. And share with others what you are doing and how it looks in your space so that your teaching community can collectively get better from your experiences also. We truly believe that we are in this together and that we are better in the company of our peers. This is especially true if you find yourself alone in this journey. We are now your community, so reach out to us through our website.

"Laying the Foundation" explains what we mean by voice and choice. We share how we came to focus on these in our teaching and why they belong in your classroom. We identify dimensions of voice and types of choice that can be infused into the teaching and learning in your classroom. We also share classroom processes and procedures that are important for creating an environment where voice and choice can thrive.

"Building a Toolkit" is full of practical tools and protocols you can teach your students that can be used across different curricula, content, and situations to bring in voice and choice. These tools can become part of a repertoire of strategies you can use to support your students in developing the skills and confidence to exercise their voice and choice muscles.

"Teaching Protocols and Task Design" focuses on instructional strategies and approaches to designing tasks for students that incorporate voice and choice.

These are universal frames for task design that can apply to a variety of disciplines.

"Assessment" cannot be forgotten as another tool to use to lift up student voice and choice in learning. In this section, we offer several different assessment strategies that centre the student in the process.

Ideas shared in "Building a Toolkit," "Teaching Protocols and Task Design," and "Assessment," all follow a common format. We will explain what the tool is in the section called "What Is It." We explore rationale for using this tool in "Why Do It? Peeling Back the Pedagogy," and explore the dimensions of voice and types of choice the tool offers. The next section, "How To Do It," explains the nuts and bolts of using the tool. In the final section, "The Tool in Practice," we present a case study where we illustrate how the tool could be used in a classroom based on our experience. These cases are presented in the first person singular to allow you to immerse yourself in the role of the teacher. We hope these fictional stories will allow you to imagine what this student-centred tool or approach might be like, positioning yourself in the role of the teacher.

Making These Resources Your Own

Throughout the book, we have shared how we would create tools and scaffolds for students in a particular discipline in our case studies and in the examples we share. We want to encourage you to make these tools and resources your own. A checklist about Canadian Immigration wouldn't be terribly helpful to you, likely. However, seeing an example of a checklist and how it could be used is hopefully the inspiration you need to incorporate this practice into your teaching. For example, you're probably already using checklists with your students. So, by sharing our specific template with you, we hope you can see how we have elevated a simple checklist to support more student voice and choice.

We hope you will take these exemplars, personalize them, hack them, and make them your own. We are open-source educators, and we want to encourage you to be the same. If you make something cool, we hope you will share it, too.

PART 1

Laying the Foundation

We hope this book will inspire you to bring more voice and choice into your classroom. We will do that by providing you with both practical activities and theoretical grounding in strategies to build more student-centred classrooms. The tools can be used in any grade and any subject, but will be most easily applicable in middle-school classrooms.

We believe passionately in student voice and choice. When we made the conscious decision to bring this to the centre of our practice, we saw the benefits right away in both student engagement and academic results. We continue to hear from former students about the impact of the way we taught. We hear about the impact of the work on their future goals as well. In these messages, we often hear regret that student voice and choice aren't always centred in all classrooms. It is our lofty goal that this book may influence more teachers to embrace this way of being.

What Is Voice?

With voice, students have an authentic say in their own learning. Students feel participatory in their learning as opposed to being an audience. Voice depends on the understanding that every student comes with experiences, thoughts, opinions, and ideas that need to be nurtured. It is important to note here that when we say every student we really do mean *every student*. We are classroom teachers first and we understand and live the complexities that are part of today's classroom settings. We have taught with neurodiverse students, EAL students, students who belong to underrepresented groups, and students with trauma. We have seen firsthand, again and again, in all these settings, that a student-centred classroom, where voice and choice are prioritized, results in the greatest long-term learning. The deepest and most meaningful learning happens when new knowledge is connected with previous knowledge. Because every student comes with different life and learning experiences, voice means that these connections are different for each child.

The most essential tool an educator has to lift up student voice is listening. Positioning yourself as chief listener is the best way to begin to explore student voice in your classroom.

Start by noticing things such as:

- What are my students' interests?
- What do my students choose to do and play during unstructured and free time?
- What are my students fascinated by? Pay close attention to what they watch on YouTube, what books they choose, what they listen to, etc.

- How do my students interact with each other?
- How do my students like to work?
- What do my students talk about? What do they talk to each other about? What do they share with me?

Attuning yourself to these questions will allow you to look for opportunities to incorporate your students' voices to bring your classroom to life.

What Is Choice?

Too often in life, we feel that we have no say in our circumstances, and this is especially true of students. It is essential to ensure that there is choice whenever possible. I might not like the alternative or the consequences of a choice but I always have a choice. Recognizing that we make hundreds of choices each day, identifying those choices, and giving students the tools to make good choices is about maximizing their agency in their own lives.

The definition of choice is obvious, but how does it live in your classroom? So much in the lives of children exists outside of their — and our — control. Bells ring and timers go off to indicate the beginning and end of most everything in our school lives, but choice is one of the most powerful tools of change.

Why is choice so powerful in the classroom? Quite simply, giving students choice gives them autonomy. We know that autonomy is necessary for human beings of all kinds. When we feel in control, we feel empowered and confident.

Choice can be small. Choice can be, "Would you like to sit at your desk or sit on the carpet and use a clipboard?" Choice can be, "Would you like to type this or handwrite it?" Small ways that you provide choice build a full sense of autonomy. All the little things you do add up to a larger picture of more engaged learners.

Choice can also be big. We can ask kids, "What topic would you like to research?" and, "Would you like to share your learning as a video, essay, or podcast?" and, "What do you want to read?" We can ask kids, "When do you want to do this project? Now, or later?" We can ask kids, "What is a reasonable due date for this work? When should you and I conference about your work?"

It is important to be obvious and intentional about choice. Teachers often hide choice as a trick to get students to be compliant but this is not about hiding the carrots in the muffin. This book is not about creating compliance. Authentic choice creates a more engaged learner who wants to be an active participant in their learning. Making this visible to students draws them into the teaching process and makes them an active participant in the way teaching and learning happens in the classroom.

This book will offer you a myriad of ways to add choice — small and big. If this is new to you, start with the small changes, but don't be afraid to jump right in.

Taking Chances

We know and fully acknowledge this is risky for the teacher. This shift requires you to move away from being "the sage on the stage." If you are reading this book, we suspect that you are already ready to reimagine your role as the teacher. You probably aren't a "desks in rows, facing forward, eyes on the teacher lecturing for an hour" kind of educator. Even so, inviting students in as participants in the instruction and assessment process requires you to let go of things and embrace ambiguity. You don't know what's going to happen when you start to let twenty-five other people have a voice in the teaching and learning in the classroom. However, with intentionality, you always know you're going to end up with something better than what you started with.

When you invite students into the design of the learning and assessment you must be transparent about accepting their ideas. As you work with your students, the work will grow and develop. To an outsider, it may look like you are allowing students to do whatever they want, but this couldn't be further from the truth. Often the students will have great ideas, but rarely do they understand the pedagogy behind what makes the ideas great. Share with them why you're using their suggestion (or why not) and tell them what makes each idea worth developing for others. Explain the research and reasoning behind an excellent resource or idea they suggested.

This is also risky for the students. Making choices takes guts. It requires them to put themselves out there and take a stand. Bringing their own interests and ideas into their classroom space makes students vulnerable. There's a risk that others won't like the same sorts of things they like. It's essential to build a classroom environment where kids feel more willing and able to take these kinds of risks. In this work, you will also build your students' capacity to use their voices and exercise their right to choice. Be prepared for students' discomfort. This often sounds like, "Can't you just tell me what to do?" Stay the course and push through this discomfort, as the ability to make choices will only improve with practice. You can support your students in developing the skills to make choices if this is not a familiar practice to them. We will share ways to do this throughout this book.

Sometimes, when students are uncomfortable or unfamiliar with the risks and rewards required in exercising voice and choice, parents and administrators can also become critically important. It is essential, when you are moving your practice forward, that you have a solid foundation in the pedagogy behind your choices and that you ground your work in your program of studies. This isn't just a "cool project." This is why we have included a section called "Peeling Back the Pedagogy" for each tool we share. This work is research-backed best practice to improve student outcomes in school and in life.

This seems like a good place to note that this work is also part of the larger journey we are all on to build equity in education. Opening up your classroom to student voice and choice opens up space for diversity, not just in terms of representation (although that is essential), but also in terms of ways of knowing and being. Through this work, we have also been able to begin decolonizing our practice, sometimes in spite of the curriculum. Voice and choice can be quite subversive.

Dimensions of Voice

We have identified twelve dimensions of voice that can be elevated in the classroom. At the beginning of this book, you will find a chart identifying which of the dimensions of voice are present in each of the tools. There is often an argument to be made for more dimensions but we have focused on those most relevant to the tools being shared.

Developing and Expressing an Opinion

Giving students an opportunity to take a stance and develop an opinion is a means to enable students to bring themselves into your classroom. This encourages students to think critically, articulate their perspectives, and make decisions that reflect their values and interests. When they have the tools and opportunities to develop and express an opinion, they experience agency in their learning, allowing them to see themselves as active participants with influence in the classroom and the world.

Communicating Academic Concepts

Finding interesting ways to draw students into their academic learning is one way to lift up student voice in the classroom. Fostering ways to communicate academic concepts enables students to express their understanding in ways that are personally meaningful and accessible to others. Giving them options for how to communicate their learning develops a stronger sense of ownership and makes learning relevant to them. When students are able to share what they know in a way that others will listen to and understand, their voice can go beyond the classroom.

Building a Skill

As we build students' skills, particularly in cross-curricular competencies and soft skills, we can help students become more confident in raising their voices in the classroom and beyond. When students develop various skills — whether in critical thinking, communication, creativity, or self-management — they gain the ability to choose paths in their learning and use their voices for greater impact.

Implementing Engagement Strategies

Being intentional about how you will bring your particular students into the work affords you an opportunity to personalize learning for your students. When we incorporate diverse engagement strategies, we support students in finding personal connections to their learning, empowering them to make choices that resonate with their interests, needs, and learning preferences.

Fostering Self-Awareness

Developing your students' capacity to be self-aware and self-reflective allows them to know themselves better and therefore make better choices in their learning. When students better understand themselves, they can feel empowered to act authentically.

Building Community

Building a safe, inclusive classroom where students feel they can be honest about who they are is an important part of this work. As mentioned, encouraging voice and choice is risky business, and investing time to build trust in the room pays off in the end. When students trust their peers and teacher, they are more willing to take ownership of their learning, share their ideas, and make choices that reflect their authentic selves.

Encouraging Independence

Empowering our students to know they can do something independently gives them confidence in themselves and their own voice. We are not encouraging you to let students learn on their own or sit compliantly at work. But, when students are given the skills to work independently and develop self-management tools, they become more confident in identifying their interests, setting goals, and selecting learning paths that align with their strengths and preferences. Independent learners feel confident in their own skills and trust that they can work by themselves to get to the next step.

Making Decisions

Being decisive is a true gift we can give our students. As students gain comfort in making decisions, they feel more confident in standing behind those decisions. When students are authentically involved in the decision-making process, they feel that their voices matter and that they have control over their educational experience.

Identifying Possibilities

Looking at a situation and being able to imagine several potential possibilities within it is a key skill students must develop. This skill is a foundational part of creative thinking and a way that students can ensure that the end result is something they are proud of. This kind of divergent thinking is essential in lifting student voices because identifying many options means there are countless opportunities for next steps.

Thinking Creatively

Creativity is a skill that requires practice. It invites students to share their unique perspectives and imagined lives, which leads to diverse and personalized ways of engaging with the classroom and the world. When students have the freedom to approach tasks creatively, they feel a sense of ownership over their learning, allowing them to make choices that align with their interests and strengths. Students will begin to understand that replication isn't the goal, and that it is preferable for work to look different depending on who has created it.

Collaborating

Collaboration gives students the opportunity to learn from diverse perspectives and strengthen their own point of view. When students work together, they not only develop interpersonal skills but also strengthen their capacity for shared responsibility and collective problem-solving, both of which are essential for fostering an inclusive classroom and society. When students collaborate, the results will be so much more interesting than they would be if the students worked in isolation. Another piece of collaboration that happens in this work is between teacher and student. Make this collaboration explicit to them and share and grow in the work with your students.

Encouraging Metacognition

Metacognition, or thinking about your own thinking, plays a key role in fostering voice and choice in the classroom by helping students become more aware of their own learning processes, preferences, and needs. When students engage in metacognitive activities, they reflect on how they learn best, what interests them, and where they may need support or challenge. This awareness is essential in empowering students to make meaningful choices in their learning and express their unique and valuable perspectives.

Types of Choice

We have also identified four types of choice that are possible. In each strategy, we explain which types of choice are present and how. While the idea of allowing students to choose whether to write a script or a short story (form) or whether to research pandas or leopards (topic) might be familiar to you, these tools will enable you to consider how to expand and support student choice in new ways.

Mode/Form

One of the most common types of choice is format or mode. This offers the student the ability to choose the product they will create or the format of their work. For example, if one student chooses to craft a comic and another chooses to write a short story to demonstrate their understanding of the elements of story, they are selecting form. Both students are demonstrating the same curricular outcomes, but the way in which they do so is different. This type of choice is important because in every classroom, we are bound to the outcomes of our provincial curriculum or state standards. Inviting students to choose their form allows them to use their own personal interests and preferences in deciding how to demonstrate the essential outcomes.

Topic/Resource

Like form and mode, topic is another common type of choice we see in classrooms. We see this, for example, when students in a classroom all participate in a research project about an animal of their choice. All students identify the habitat, life cycles, and interesting facts about an animal, but which animal they choose is up to them. They may also have opportunities to choose the resources they consult as they learn. Students might be choosing what books, websites, videos, podcasts, or other texts they use to support them in their learning. As with mode and form, this allows students to bring their own interests into their learning, selecting a topic that matters to them.

Outcome

We can invite students to choose which curricular goals their work is tied to. This is probably the most complex type of choice but it can also lead to the greatest rewards. Providing this type of choice allows students to define their own goals within the confines of the curriculum, pursuing paths that better align with their interests, and demonstrating their learning in ways that are meaningful and authentic to them. This empowers students to a greater depth of understanding about what they are learning and why, which leads to more self-directed and reflective learners. When students are given the option to choose their learning outcomes, they need to think critically about the best way to approach the task which leads to problem-solving and planning beyond that allowed in following a set task. For example, when students are demonstrating their understanding of how authors use techniques and elements to enhance a message, the students could choose to demonstrate a learner outcome about characterization, plot, topic and theme, or perspective. This type of personalization can also allow students to see the connections between what they are learning and their own lives, increasing intrinsic motivation. As students see the results of their decisions, they gain a sense of achievement and agency, which creates a virtuous cycle of growth and engagement.

Time and Sequence

We can provide students with opportunities to choose when they do their work and in which order. This type of choice matters because it gives students the flexibility to manage their learning in a way that best suits their needs, preferences, and pace. Gaining control over time encourages self-regulation. We all know that not everyone learns at the same pace. Students can work at a pace that feels comfortable to them, which can reduce stress and frustration for those who need more time and prevent boredom for those who can advance more rapidly. Additionally, allowing students to sequence their work in a way that makes sense to them can foster curiosity and creativity, allowing them to make connections between ideas and experiences that we might not have envisioned.

Laying the Foundation

It is essential, in a student-centred classroom, to lay a strong foundation of trust and respect. Classroom climate and community matter in this work even more than they already do in a more teacher-centred classroom. The activities that follow are designed to help build the necessary foundation for student voice and choice.

"Getting to Know You" activities are the hallmark (and bane?) of first days everywhere. What is different about the activities we share here is that they are focused on building a foundation in your classroom that prioritizes student voice and choice. So much of the groundwork that creates an environment where students feel safe to take the creative risks necessary to make real, authentic choices in their learning can be established with clear and thoughtful activities and procedures at the beginning of the year. If you are reading this book and it is not August, it is not too late. You can start this work whenever you are ready and build from there.

Choice-based activities provide valuable insight into students' interests, preferences, and decision-making processes. Allowing students to choose how they engage — whether through modes (drawing, writing, verbal sharing), topics, or group configurations — gives teachers a window into their personalities, strengths, and passions. Offering choice gives teachers the opportunity to observe which preferences resonate most with their students. When you learn what choices your students gravitate toward, you are learning about your students. These preferences can guide future task design and content differentiation. Self-Determination Theory emphasizes the importance of autonomy in fostering intrinsic motivation. When students feel they have agency in their learning, they are more likely to engage deeply and persist in tasks (Ryan and Deci, 1985). When students see their choices reflected in the classroom it builds trust and investment in their learning experience.

As you begin to offer choice in your classroom your students will have to deal with uncertainty. This is an inevitable part of learning, especially when fostering critical thinking and creativity. Developing resilience in the face of uncertainty aligns with research on growth mindset and constructivist learning theories. Carol Dweck's work in growth mindset highlights that students who see challenges and uncertainty as opportunities to grow are more likely to persevere and succeed (Dweck, 2016). This directly connects to Vygotsky's Constructivist Theory, which shows that learning through problem-solving and discovery, grappling with uncertainty, fosters deeper understanding and critical thinking (Vygotsky, 1978). "Getting to Know You" activities can gently challenge students to navigate ambiguity in a low-stakes way. These tasks can reveal how students handle open-ended activities, collaborate under unclear parameters, or manage the discomfort of not knowing "the right answer." Teachers can observe which students dive into the challenge enthusiastically, who needs reassurance, and who prefers structure. This knowledge also informs how to scaffold future tasks. As students practice engaging with uncertainty in a supportive environment, they become more comfortable taking risks and exploring new ideas.

Sharing ideas and stepping out of comfort zones are crucial for growth, yet they require a classroom culture rooted in safety and respect. These early activities normalize making mistakes, celebrating effort and the modeling of vulnerability, and can set the tone for mutual trust. Students begin to see the classroom as a safe space to share authentically, where their contributions — whether polished or imperfect — are valued. Over time, this culture translates to greater participation and deeper engagement.

Collaboration is not an inherent skill; it must be nurtured through deliberate practice. These activities offer the perfect starting point for cultivating teamwork. They require group problem-solving or shared decision-making and introduce the principles of active listening, compromise, and collective effort. They give teachers an opportunity to observe group dynamics — who takes the lead, who hangs back, and how students interact — and use this information to inform future groupings or targeted support. Students begin to appreciate the value of diverse perspectives and experiences through the rewards of working together. This foundation is crucial for more complex collaborative tasks later in the year.

A meta-analysis of classroom management and climate (Marzano et al., 2003) found that fostering positive relationships, building student trust, and creating an inclusive environment directly correlate with higher academic achievement and engagement. Activities that emphasize student voice, choice, and collaboration are key strategies for establishing this foundation. Research consistently supports the use of student-centred, choice-driven, and collaborative strategies to create a classroom environment where students feel safe, valued, and empowered. These principles are not just anecdotal; they are grounded in decades of educational theory and practice.

What we have noticed in our classrooms and as leaders in schools is that all teachers recognize the importance of this work, but not everyone knows how to do it, especially in the face of the many other demands that are present in schools. What follows are a few of the ways that you can meaningfully start building a culture that prioritizes voice and choice.

Soft Entry Activity Options

Having activities for students to engage in as soon as they enter the classroom accomplishes two things. First, it gives students something to do during a time that can otherwise feel awkward, particularly when they don't know one another. Second, it allows you as the teacher to observe a few things and start documenting what you are learning about your students, such as:

- To which activities does each student gravitate?
- What are the students doing as they participate? Are they chatting with others? Engaging quietly? Disengaged?
- Are there certain activities that are very popular? What's happening here?
- Are there certain activities that are not at all popular? Why?

We have many different activities that are our "go to" activities for these soft entry moments:

- LEGO: LEGO allows students to use their hands and is a familiar medium for many kids of different ages.
- Jigsaw puzzles: You can find many puzzles at second-hand stores. Jigsaw puzzles are often low-risk, easy activities many people can engage in at the same time.
- Group coloring posters: You can find online and print or purchase large coloring sheets or posters that multiple people can work on at the same time. Larger posters encourage collaboration, as opposed to single sheets.
- Easy games that most people know, like Uno or Jenga: Select games that are easy to play and don't require much time to learn rules. Uno is always a classic in our classrooms.
- Playdough: No kid is too old for Playdough. Put a few containers out on tables and watch what happens!
- Rubik's Cubes and other tactile puzzles: Rubik's Cubes keep hands busy, which can lower stress levels. There are other tactile puzzles made of metal, wood, or plastic that can be purchased as well.
- Illustrated books and comic books: Having some high-quality illustrated texts (picture books) and comic books that students can read alone or with a partner or in small groups can support students who enjoy reading and stories.
- Toys (such as magnatiles, blocks, tinker toys, cars and roads, Snap Circuits, etc.): Toys that involve building or manipulating and allow for multiple means of expression are the best kind.

You can allow students to explore these soft entry activities freely. It's also interesting to put a timer on and ask students to switch activities after the timer rings. You can tell students, "Choose a new activity and sit with different people," as a way to observe students in different settings and also observe classroom dynamics.

PowerPoint Pitch Party

This activity capitalizes on a once-popular social media trend but is actually timeless in nature. Students, alone or in groups, create a slideshow pitch presentation on a topic of their choice. You can offer design constraints and the topics can be serious or light-hearted. The most important reminder is that they must be school-appropriate. The pitch element is essential as students are creating a persuasive presentation for their peers. For example:

- In three slides maximum, choose the best class pet.
- You have zero budget. What should we do for a one-hour class party?
- Dedicate your learning today to a person of your choice.

Photo Scavenger Hunt

Give students a list of things to find and photograph. Better yet, generate a list as a class. Have them work in teams or alone. This is a great opportunity to observe who works with whom, who has no one to work with, and who chooses to work alone. You can see how your students respond to competition and time-sensitive tasks in a low-risk environment.

Some options for leveling up this activity include:

- Everyone must finish and there can be no repeat photos.
- Each group has a different part of the list and they aren't done until the class has a complete list.
- Use vocabulary words or concepts.

You can find great ideas for scavenger hunt items by searching online.

STEM Challenges

STEM challenges are activities that encourage thinking in science, technology, engineering, and mathematics. They are collaborative, open-ended problem-solving tasks. A key feature of these types of tasks is that they have specific design constraints to force creative thinking. This can be in material type, amount, time, design details, etc. There is no right way to do this type of task. Some of our favorite group challenges are:

- Spaghetti Marshmallow Tower: Each group gets dried spaghetti and mini marshmallows. They must build the tallest freestanding tower they can.
- Found Materials Bridge: Build the longest bridge that can hold the most weight, using paper and masking tape.
- Egg Drop: Design and build a parachute that allows an egg to be safely dropped from the greatest height.
- The Unmeltable Ice Cube: Build a container that will keep an ice cube frozen for the longest time (or for the duration of the song "Ice, Ice, Baby" by Vanilla Ice).

TASK Party

This is a kind of participatory performance art originally created by artist Oliver Herring. In a TASK party, you put a bunch of tasks written on pieces of paper in a basket or bin. Set out a table full of materials that students can use to build with, such as a variety of papers, markers, tape, scissors, string, glue, pipe cleaners, popsicle sticks, cardboard, and recycled and found items like bottle caps, cardboard tubes, plastic bags, etc. Invite students to pull a task out of the bin, and then complete the task. When they are done, they can choose another task from the bin to carry out. An optional step is to have students add another task to the bin when they pull one out.

TASK parties give you an opportunity to observe students playfully engaging in low-stakes risk-taking. Many of the tasks require students to step outside of their comfort zone and engage in something slightly silly and take a risk to have fun, such as:

- Make a crown and wear it around, acting like royalty.
- Create a new superhero.
- Make the tallest hat you can.
- Make a birthday card for the person in the room whose birthday is next.
- Give everyone you meet a high-five.
- Lie down on the floor until someone asks you what you are doing.
- Perform a marriage ceremony for two inanimate objects.

Other ideas for TASK parties can be found online.

Communal Experience of Making and Sharing Food

The act of preparing and sharing food can involve a sequence of cooperative actions that naturally fosters connection and unity. Whether it's chopping vegetables, stirring a pot, or setting the table, these activities encourage interaction and cooperation, promoting a sense of teamwork and shared purpose. Food often serves as a universal language, transcending cultural or language barriers. Sharing a meal invites conversation and interaction in a natural, unpressured way, giving students a chance to connect as human beings beyond typical roles or expectations. Coming together around food symbolizes a sense of togetherness and community. The informal nature of cooking and eating together fosters open communication. It's less structured than a formal meeting or discussion, so it can lead to more relaxed, authentic conversations. People feel more comfortable expressing themselves and sharing personal stories or ideas.

Students can work together to prepare ingredients, follow instructions, and support each other throughout the cooking process. When they collaborate on making food, they practice communication, problem-solving, and negotiation — key skills for any collaborative endeavor. Cooking offers numerous opportunities for students to make choices, such as selecting ingredients, deciding on presentation styles, or adapting recipes to their taste. It also requires students to engage with uncertainty, take risks, and experiment with new ideas. Whether it's trying out a new flavor combination or adapting a recipe, students are encouraged to step outside their comfort zones and be creative. The entire aspect of cooking and sitting down together to share a meal reinforces the idea that taking risks and working together are part of a larger, meaningful experience. Sharing the results of their cooking in a group reinforces the idea that collaboration and risk-taking can lead to positive outcomes. And by bringing together diverse food traditions and celebrating the varied backgrounds of students, you can open the door to discussions about identity, culture, and shared experiences, which are important for building an inclusive and respectful classroom community.

While not every classroom has access to a kitchen, even something as simple as a potluck can reap the benefits of this community-building activity and help set a positive tone for the year.

Community Service Project

A community service project can play a powerful role in building a collaborative classroom that prioritizes student voice and choice, as it provides students with opportunities to take ownership of their learning while engaging in meaningful work. If you allow students to have a voice in the direction of a project, whether identifying the issue or determining how they want to contribute to addressing it, you will contribute to their sense of ownership and agency. Larger-scale community service projects often require students to work together to achieve a common goal, encouraging collaboration from the outset. This naturally cultivates an understanding that everyone's input is valuable. Students learn to listen to each other, share ideas, and respect diverse perspectives. When students are involved in a community service project, they're asked to make real, authentic choices that matter to the community and affect the project's success. These decisions are not abstract or hypothetical but connected to tangible outcomes. The real-world nature of these choices fosters a sense of responsibility and accountability. Because the project is meaningful, students understand that their voice and ideas can shape outcomes, helping them see the impact of their decisions. As a result, they feel more confident in making authentic choices in their learning across all subjects, knowing that their opinions and contributions are valued.

There are many examples of large-scale projects, and many of the tools in this book could be used to identify a focus and create an action plan. But you can definitely start small. Invite your students to commit to one action, such as picking up a piece of trash, and then ask them to scale their idea. What could two people do? Can they get a friend to commit? What could the class do? Could each student create a thirty-second pitch for their idea? Have the class choose one for the year or each month. If you teach at a school that commits to community service projects, like collecting for the local food bank, invite your students to research the area of greatest need and create school-wide advertising to drive donations. The opportunities, curricular connections, and benefits to your students are almost limitless. One of our favorite, small-scale projects inspired by an Edutopia social media post (2023) found us partnering with a local coffee shop to spread a little positivity by decorating sleeves for coffee cups.

Class Norm Creation/Community Rules

Creating class norms at the beginning of the year helps build a collaborative classroom by giving students a voice in shaping the learning environment. When students contribute to establishing expectations for respect and communication, they feel more invested in maintaining a positive and supportive atmosphere. This sense of ownership fosters a safe space for students to take creative risks and make authentic choices without fear of judgment. Clear norms around respect and openness encourage students to share ideas, collaborate, and experiment, knowing their contributions will be valued. Every group has norms. Make sure yours are intentional.

A simple strategy to create class norms uses some of the tools in this book. Use "Brainstorming Possibilities" to come up with a list of words that describe success in a variety of school situations. You could then use a "Live Draft" or "Heat Mapping" to narrow down your list. The end result would be a list of words that describe students in your class or grade when they are at their very best. During each class, have the students choose the best norms from the curated list to describe what the classroom should look and sound like during the day's task.

Class Rituals

Designing class rituals that encourage risk-taking and build community helps create a collaborative classroom by establishing consistent, supportive practices where students feel safe to express themselves and take risks. Some examples of rituals might include:

- Showing appreciation for sharing or presentations: Whenever someone shares or presents in class, everyone participates in the applause. This is how we say thank you for being brave and sharing and it doesn't matter if we liked the presentation; we still applaud as a way to say thank you.
- Acknowledging arrivals and departures: During morning meeting or circle time, introduce any new student and give them a small welcome gift, like a bookmark or pencil. This is especially meaningful if it is something that everyone in the class got on their first day. It is also important to recognize a student leaving through a small activity or ritual, like having everyone write a note for a card.
- Recognizing others' accomplishments: Invite students to submit salutes, shoutouts, and shares to you each week. At the end of the week pin them up on your bulletin board or share them in a class meeting.
- Failure celebration: One of our favorite bulletin board displays was an interactive guessing game. Lines from students' first drafts were posted on one side and the same lines from their final drafts was posted on the other side. The first student who was able to correctly match the drafts won a prize. What we love about this is that it celebrates growth and improvement. Another bulletin board showcased all the weird and misshapen first attempts at knitting a small square from a fashion class. The title was "This is what it looks like when you learn something new…" These celebrations normalized vulnerability and creative exploration, fostering an environment where students share ideas and try new things without fear of judgment.

Creative Thinking Warmups

Creative thinking warmups are grounded in theatrical improvisation, accepting what is presented, without judgment, and offering up something in return. In 1978, in Calgary, Keith Johnstone invented Theatresports™, a competitive performance of improvisation games. These "games" have since made their way around the world and into a variety of industries. The basic principles of any of these activities involve accepting and building upon the ideas of others. This is summed up in the phrase, "Yes, and…" A common misconception in improvisation is that it requires unique and extraordinary ideas, but the best improvisers behave in expected ways. If the telephone rings, don't hide behind the couch; answer the phone. Participation is spontaneous and immediate. Students should be encouraged to focus on listening and responding in authentic ways. The games themselves are widely available and are often passed down through oral tradition, from class to class.

Participating in improvisation creates positive experiences in group collaboration, self-efficacy, and divergent thinking. Improvisational theatre training can improve divergent thinking (Felsman et al., 2019). Research into the long-held anecdotal beliefs in the benefits of improv training has also provided new findings that it can increase uncertainty tolerance relative to other social interactions. Doing just twenty minutes of improv can increase creativity, well-being, and our ability to tolerate uncertainty, which are all great reasons to have some fun in your class. Of particular note is research that shows that doing improv is associated with reductions in social anxiety in adolescents (Felsman et al., 2020).

A simple internet search will yield a myriad of improv games that you can try in your classes. We especially love the Stoke Deck, a collection of twenty-eight activities in a card deck format or accessible through a website, curated and designed by Taylor Cone, Tania Anaissie, and Ashish Goel at the Stanford d.school in 2014. When selecting a game to try in your class, consider your ultimate goal.

These exercises can also become observational formative assessments as you note which students are struggling and which have ease. You can differentiate this task when you are assigning the topics by designing a wide variety of challenges and by assigning them based on student need.

One element that can by effectively incorporated is the arbitrary awarding of points. It adds to the competitive spirit and feeds into the game-like nature of improv activities. Depending on your class composition, you might also consider allowing student judges. While the awarding of points pulls students out of the collaborative nature of the activity, it can be a great fit for those who struggle with the immediacy of thinking that these activities require. Points can be taken as seriously (or not) as your class would like but the chaos that results from rewarding a great idea or connection with 1,000 points is nothing short of joyful. This is a great way to remind you to have fun with this work!

Here are a few of our favorite activities to get your class working together and thinking creatively.

Fortunately/Unfortunately

This is a beginning improv game that helps students create interesting stories by thinking quickly and creatively and listening carefully to others. The goal of the game is for the group to tell a coherent story, with each student contributing one line at a time. It works as follows:

1. A leader will begin the story with one establishing sentence.
2. Then every line must alternate between "Fortunately…" and "Unfortunately…".

It is easy to adapt this to a wide variety of subject-specific contexts. For example:

- English Language Arts: Encourage students to follow the elements of plot structure.

- Math: Incorporate problem-solving and mental math in the storytelling.
- Science: Use scientific vocabulary.
- Social Studies: Set the story during the time period being studied and require historical accuracy.

Reflection Questions

- Which requirements were the easiest to meet? Which requirements were the hardest? This can reveal areas for enrichment or review.
- If you are awarding points, a discussion about your judgments can provoke excellent critical thinking. This can happen in the moment or at the end.

Blobs and Lines

Students are prompted to either line up in some particular order (by birthday, for example) or gather in "blobs" based on something they have in common (similar shoes, for example). What's great about this game is that it helps students quickly discover things they have in common. It's also ridiculously easy: Students don't have to come up with anything clever, and they can respond to every question without thinking too hard about it.

Here are some sample general prompts you can use for this game:

- Line up in alphabetical order by your first names.
- Line up in alphabetical order by your last names.
- Line up in order of your birthdays, from January 1 through December 31.
- Line up in order of how many languages you speak.
- Gather with people who have the same eye color as you.
- Gather with people who get to school in the same way as you (car, bus, walk).
- Choose one of three blobs about how you spent your summer:
  - Watching movies, Netflix (etc.), or YouTube.
  - Working, creating, or building.
  - Travelling or visiting friends or family.

Blobs and lines can also be used to learn and review curricular content. Here are some sample curricular prompts you can use for this game using notes on cards given to each student:

- Social Studies: Give students different roles and sort them into a social hierarchy, or give them different functions and sort them into the branches of government.
- Science: Select animals and sort them into different habitats.
- English Language Arts: Give students lines from your novel study that describe different characters and sort them into which characters they describe. Subdivide into direct or indirect characterization.
- Math: Give each student a fraction and ask them to organize themselves from greatest to least.

Reflection Questions

- Was this activity difficult? Why?
- What is something new you learned about a classmate?
- Which topics were the hardest? Why?

Category, Category, Die

This can be a great way to get kids brainstorming possible topics. It works as follows:

1. Circle up.
2. Choose a category such as: Types of trees, cereal brands, literary devices, words related to anatomy (or whatever topic you're studying).
3. Go around the circle with each person giving a word from the category (e.g., maple, Trix, allusions, or liver).
4. When someone can't think of a word or repeats one that's been said, they're out (dead)!

Tip: Add another category moving in the opposite direction for an extra challenge!

This game can also be great for reviewing academic vocabulary or overarching concepts. For example, you could give students a concept you have been learning about and ask each student to think of a unique term or example that connects with the concept. For example:

- English Language Arts: Names of characters, literary terms, parts of speech, book titles within a certain genre.
- Social Studies: Vocabulary words connected with the Youth Criminal Justice Act, Explorers of Canada.
- Science: Vocabulary words related to freshwater systems, types of simple machines, characteristics of an ecosystem, periodic table of elements.
- Math: Examples of problem types (addition, subtraction), fractions (irregular, mixed), times tables, geometric shapes.

Reflection Questions
- What made this activity challenging?
- What skills did you need to stay alive?

Yes, Let's!

This game reinforces a basic principle of improv: Accepting what's given. Here's the procedure:

1. Divide your class into groups.
2. Ask the first group to take the "stage."
3. One player in the group starts by saying, "Let's [activity]!" and then performs the activity (e.g., "Let's go shopping" or "Let's do our homework" or "Let's go surfing," etc.)
4. Then all the other players on stage support the action by jumping in and saying, "Yes, let's!"
5. Everyone then proceeds to mime the activity together until another person in the group starts a new "Let's [activity]!"
6. Everyone else says, "Yes, let's!" and proceeds to perform the activity. Encourage the players to always be physically active.
7. This pattern continues until everyone has had a chance to suggest an activity.
8. After the first group finishes, ask the second group to take the stage and do the same.

Reflection Questions

- Was this activity difficult? Why or why not?
- Did it make things easier/smoother knowing that you had to accept the activity?
- Did you feel more connected with your group by the end of the activity?
- How would this activity be different if you were allowed to "block" the suggestion?

This Is Not a____, It's a_____.

The goal of the game is to make an object into something it is not by using actions and descriptive language.

1. After choosing an object, hold it and say, "This is not a [whatever it really is]. It's a [give it a different function]." For example, "This is not a spatula. It's a stake to hold up small plants in my garden."
2. Pass the item to the next student, or allow for a volunteer, who then comes up with another use. "This is not a garden stake, it's a cat-scarer to keep my cat off my couch."
3. You can continue until everyone has had a turn or you can play until there are no new ideas.

Details can be added depending on your setting and your goals. For example, specify that your description must have an adjective or a preposition. It is especially fun if students also act out the object in use.

Reflection Questions

- Was this activity difficult? Why or why not?
- What skills are most important for success in this game?
- Could you connect this activity to a classroom skill?

Headbands

This is based on the board game Hedbanz and is also a variation on the classic game Twenty Questions. It can be easily adapted for any subject or age level, especially as it can use both words and pictures.

1. Each person in a group wears a headband with a card stuck in it so that they can't see what is on the card. A sticky note on the forehead works just as well.
2. Each card has a picture and a label for what the item is.
3. Each person needs to ask their teammates yes/no questions to try to figure out what item is on their card. "Am I an animal? Can I walk? Do I have teeth?"
4. Using their teammates' answers, they eventually guess what the item is.

Headbands is also a great game to incorporate academic content. For example:
- English Language Arts: Topics could be literary devices, characters from a class novel, etc.
- Science: Topics could include scientific vocabulary.
- Math: Topics could include numbers, equations, expressions, and academic vocabulary.

- Social Studies: Topics could include famous people, big ideas, and current events.

Reflection Questions

- Was this activity difficult? Why or why not?
- What skills are most important for success in this game?

PART 2

Building a Toolkit

In order for students to engage in work where they are actively making choices that matter, they need to build a set of strategies and tools to support them in this work. Giving students the ability to bring their own topics, ideas, and preferences into the classroom should be simple, right? In reality, it's often overwhelming and risky for both kids and adults. How often have you sat in a staff meeting or team planning session where no one shared? It takes a lot of guts to bring something you care about into a communal space.

Giving students tools and scaffolds to bring voice and choice into their learning can make this risk a little less scary. Teaching them how to identify their interests and passions and then finding ways to incorporate that into their day-to-day learning requires forethought and intentionality. Otherwise, it is just talking about stuff you like and while that is a key part of relationship and community building that is not what we are talking about here. Without intentionality, the depth of the work and the impact of incorporating voice and choice into learning will be limited.

Another reason why having a toolkit of strategies and methods students can use to bring themselves into their learning is to support organization and focus in the work. It's easy to see how having twenty-five different things happening in the classroom at once could be chaotic and scattered. A toolkit of common protocols the students know and can use creates a system where students can all be working towards the same end result but with flexibility and generosity. Once students know the protocol, they can use it again and again with different content and topics. When you are incorporating voice and choice into your classroom, whether it is for a whole unit design or a portion of a lesson, ask yourself what the structure is and what routines you need to support this. Teach the routines first.

Good classroom management is essential for student choice to be successful. This is not a book about classroom management, but in order to free up the time and space for students to explore their own decisions and ideas, solid routines and procedures must be in place. If you are finding that voice and choice isn't working, consider your classroom management before you throw out the tool.

Some classroom routines we have found to be important in making this work follow here. In all of these routines, consider how you can free yourself up to collaborate with students and help them work through their ideas, rather than managing off-task behaviors, student interactions, and administrative distractions.

Answering the Phone

What do you do when the phone rings in your classroom? In a student-centred classroom, you are continually engaging with learners in small groups and one to one. Answering the phone disrupts this. Even when teaching a whole class lesson, answering the phone can make the difference between having a focused, engaged class and a room full of side conversations. Teach your students how to manage phone disruptions. We have found the following script to be very helpful: "Hello, student speaking. Mrs. Vandertoorn is teaching right now. Is this an emergency or can I take a message?" Obviously, if it is an emergency, you will take the call, but another student can tell James to go get his lunch from the office just as easily as you can. Teach students to do this in a calm way and emphasize that it should not disrupt learning. Whoever is closest to the phone answers it.

Entering and Exiting the Classroom

Human beings have biological needs. They need to go to the bathroom and stay hydrated. Of course, we know sometimes students can use these needs as an excuse for disengaging from their work. Have an explicit conversation with your students to support them in understanding how to appropriately decide when to leave the class. For example, during the middle of an explanation of a subject or task is not a good time but during a transition from one activity to another is. Support your students in asking for what they need so that they aren't using going to the washroom as an excuse for a movement break. It's important to have this conversation with your students in the beginning and again and again through the school year. Let them know you trust them to make these decisions and that if they give you a reason not to trust them, the privilege of deciding for themselves can be removed.

One of the best ways we have to manage entering and exiting the room is hall passes. We have two lanyards hanging on the wall by the door and students grab one when they need to leave the room. With older students, and depending on your school's requirements, we may also have a sign-out book. Each student gives you a signal, such as making a "W" with her hands, to show she needs the washroom. With younger students, we know of a teacher who has two stuffed animals and when a student leaves the room, she places a stuffed animal on her chair to show she's left. When students are working in groups, we also reinforce the importance of letting your group know where you are as a tool to increase accountability.

Systems like these give you the information you need — knowing who is out of the room and why — but don't take too much of your time away from teaching and working with students.

Setting Up the Space

Be intentional and flexible in how you design your space. Behavior challenges can arise when students choose their own seats, as Bicard, Ervin, and Bicard (2012) discovered, noticing that "disruptive behavior during group seating occurred at twice the rate when students choose their seats than when the teacher chose. During individual seating, disruptive behavior occurred more than three times as often when the students choose their seats" (p. 407). This is not an argument against student choice in seating but rather for intentional design.

There are also significant benefits to allowing choice in seating. This includes promoting student autonomy, collaborative learning, building a sense of belonging, and leveraging peer relationships to support learning.

One strategy to balance these seemingly conflicting outcomes is to invite students into the process of seating plan creation. We use sticky notes and have each student write their name and the names of three peers they would like to sit with. Sometimes there are additional parameters, such as including someone you haven't sat with before, or making sure that one of the people must be of the opposite gender. We make it clear that this is not a guarantee that students will be seated with these people and that we also have input. One of our classroom norms is that everyone will work willingly and kindly with everyone in the class throughout the year. Our students do not have to be friends but they do have to be kind. We also make it clear that any seating plan is for now but not for forever.

We then use our sticky notes to create a seating plan. This establishes the group for collaborative work. During individual work there are flexible seating options and breakout spaces available so that students can change their seats.

A great benefit of this method is that it also allows you to learn a little bit more about your students and manage classroom dynamics. Whose name is on all the lists? Whose name is on no one's list? Who only has one name to write down? Who was on many students' lists previously but is no longer on many? Who hangs out with one group but puts the names of other students on their list? This is valuable information to a classroom teacher.

Independent Work Routines

One of the most important routines we teach in a student-centred classroom involves the expectations around independent work time. These routines "foster students' development of metacognition, motivation and strategic action. These underlying learning competencies improve students' academic, social, emotional and career outcomes" (Brenner, 2022). When students are working on projects where they have a vested interest in the work, engagement is more likely, but we know that setting up strong expectations around this time is important for success. We think you can all relate to this scenario: You're working on a project with your class. It's a big project, taking weeks of class time. Everyone in the class is working away busily, typing on computers, quietly focused. You're expecting great things. And then, at the end of the work, you pull open one student's project only to find it blank. What were they doing that whole time? When you talk to them, they tell you that they were stuck on one part of the project and didn't know how to move on. You're frustrated because you think the student should have just asked you what to do.

Establishing solid routines for independent work can help you avoid some of this heartache. In our middle school classrooms, we established something called "Starbucks Time," which is not our invention and can be found from multiple sources online. "Starbucks Time" invites students to act as they would in a cafe full of strangers: Open their laptops, put headphones on if they want, and focus on the work. We always say, "Don't be that weird guy at Starbucks who talks to strangers." A very simple way we indicate a shift to "Starbucks Time" is by turning down the lights. When the lights go down, so do the voices, and students get to work.

We also implemented something at the beginning of an independent work time we call "Triage." As in a hospital, the purpose of "Triage" is to identify those who are bleeding from their metaphorical femoral artery. A student in need of triage is a student who cannot move forward without something specific from the teacher. This is a few minutes of time at the beginning of work when we invite students who need something from us — a question, something they are stuck on, or a resource they need — to come and get what they need before we move into uninterrupted work time.

One of the simplest ways to nurture students' independence is to introduce them to the power of online tutorials. Platforms like YouTube, Khan Academy, and even free coding sites like Scratch offer accessible, step-by-step guidance on everything from creating a persuasive infographic to exploring the basics of quadratic equations. By teaching students how to find and use these resources effectively, you reinforce a lifelong skill: the ability to seek out knowledge on their own terms.

Supporting students in this process can start with showing them how to evaluate the quality of a tutorial. Encourage them to look for clear explanations, reliable sources, and creators who explain why something works, not just how to do it. Creative projects such as learning to draw in perspective or edit a short film can thrive when students feel confident choosing tutorials that align with their goals and push their critical thinking.

To make this approach successful, consider modeling this process for your class. Many of our students seem to live their lives online but we were surprised at how few knew to pause a video to complete a step before resuming play for the next instruction. You might show students how to search effectively using specific terms, review a video for its usefulness, or cross-check information when it's more complex. Pair this with clear expectations: ask students to briefly explain what they've learned from a tutorial or how they plan to apply it. This ensures that they aren't just passively consuming content but are actually engaging critically with what they're learning. By embedding this process in independent work routines, you'll build confidence and creativity.

Managing Interruptions

Create a norm in your classroom that teaching time is important and should not be disrupted. Let your students know that when you're working with them one on one or in a small group it is sacred teaching time. You want their undivided attention and you want to give them your undivided attention. They should only interrupt for essential needs. Make sure students know what they should be doing now and what they should be doing next so that you can teach without interruption. And hold your boundaries. If a student interrupts, you can shake your head no and continue with your small group. Don't interrupt a conference to respond to a request to get a drink. Let a student answer the phone and don't look over expectantly; trust that they can follow the routine.

Structure and routines are essential to free you up to actually teach, because in a student-centred classroom you are rarely standing in front of the class delivering a whole class lecture and you are even less often sitting at your desk working on something else. As you read about each tool, pay careful attention to the "Tool in Practice" section and you can see how the teacher is actively engaging with students and offering individual, small-group, and whole-class instruction.

Solving a Problem

Think ahead about the problems your students might run into. What resources might they need? What roadblocks could they run into? Then think about how you can design your classroom in such a way that students can solve their own problems.

One system we used in our own classrooms is a "One Stop Shop" for resources to support the work. We used milk crates and hanging folders with tabs to show what each folder contained. In the folders we kept extra copies of resources, flat sheets, and instructions. For example, if a student wanted to make a podcast, we had a flat sheet for "How to Record a Podcast" where they could access "just in time" instructions for what they needed. Another way we've seen these types of resources organized in classrooms is in pocket charts hanging on the wall. QR codes are also a great way to give students "just in time" access to these types of resources. And, of course, if your students are comfortable in digital environments, such resources can also be stored digitally, such as in Google Classroom or on a class website.

Anchor charts are another resource students can use to solve their own problems, with common questions and answers related to the task or the work posted in a public space.

The individual problems your students might run into are really dependent on the task, but thinking of those problems ahead of time and giving students support in solving those problems themselves minimizes disruptions.

Shifting the Thinking around "What Is Teaching?"

Something that we have come up against, even in our own practice, is that in a student-centred environment it can sometimes feel as if you aren't actually teaching. A shift to a student-centred classroom means you are rarely lecturing in front of the whole class, as you understand teaching and learning to involve much more than just knowledge transmission.

We are indebted to the Reggio Emilia approach to learning and the understanding of the hundred languages of children (Malaguzzi and Gandini). If there are hundreds of different ways children learn and communicate their learning, then so too must there be hundreds of ways to teach. We must open ourselves up to these possibilities. This is an exciting prospect; as we become attuned to the needs of our students, possibilities emerge.

In these possibilities, however, we do acknowledge that there will sometimes be discomfort when a clear path doesn't immediately emerge as the way forward. There will be discomfort as you no longer have a lesson plan that someone else wrote to guide your decisions. There will be discomfort for students who are used to worksheets and questions with binary answers. There will be discomfort for students who have never really been asked for their input into instructional design before. There will be discomfort for students in places where compliance has been expected and collaboration has not been encouraged.

Get comfortable with the discomfort. Lean on the tools to support you in knowing that there *is* a clear path forward, but that the clear path is in the structure, not the content. And know that as you and your students become more practiced at making decisions, they will become easier to make. Remind yourselves that if it feels too easy, nobody's learning. And that the joy and benefit in the student-centred classroom is absolutely that *everyone* is learning.

Each tool that is included in this section of the book is a protocol you can use with students to help them develop the skills and capacities to make good choices and become fully involved partners in their own learning.

AI for Voice and Choice

What Is It?

Rapidly advancing technology presents us with opportunities to expand our practice and our students' learning. One area that is currently blowing up is the use of AI. Our world of technology is changing so quickly that it seems foolhardy to suggest specific platforms that may or may not be around when you are reading this. The ideas we will share in this section will be generic so as to be platform-agnostic. A quick internet search will lead to a wide variety of currently useful tools but the principles shared here will apply regardless of which specific AI tool you are utilizing. At the time of printing, some of the most popular AI tools in education are ChatGPT, Diffit, Magic School AI, Microsoft Copilot, and Brisk AI.

We believe that there is tremendous potential within this technology to support voice and choice for teachers and students. Feedback for growth is one such area and will be addressed specifically in the "Peer Feedback" section. AI tools can be used to give students detailed feedback at various stages of their work, allowing them to improve and grow as they go. When creating presentations or projects, students can select the medium they prefer, with AI tools supporting their chosen format. AI can also facilitate collaboration among students, allowing them to work together on projects, share ideas, and provide peer feedback. By using AI platforms that enable real-time collaboration, students can communicate effectively and learn from each other. AI tools can also challenge students to think creatively and critically at precisely their point of understanding. This not only nurtures critical thinking but also invites them to express their unique viewpoints.

Why Do It? Peeling Back the Pedagogy

AI tools can adapt to individual student needs, creating personalized learning experiences that cater to varying levels of interest and ability. This personalization can deepen students' ownership over their learning, as they are willing to engage more deeply with material that resonates with them. When students feel that their unique voices and choices are valued, their motivation to learn increases significantly. AI can also be used to translate and differentiate texts across subjects. In today's increasingly diverse and complex classrooms, AI is a valuable tool that allows teachers to leverage their subject knowledge and understanding of their students to create individual programs and resources that would not have been possible before AI.

Incorporating AI into the classroom also prepares students for a future where technology will play an even more significant role in their lives. By familiarizing them with AI tools, we equip them with skills that are increasingly relevant in today's job market. Understanding how to leverage technology for learning and collaboration is an essential competency for future success.

With any new technology there is a wide debate about its use and integration into education. Teachers who choose to teach with AI are tasking themselves with the responsibility to be critical users and to teach critical use skills to their students. You cannot abdicate this responsibility.

How to Do It

Here are a few ways that AI can support student voice and choice in different disciplines.

Math Class

1. Choice Boards: AI platforms can create personalized choice boards where students select tasks or projects that align with their interests.
2. Project-Based Learning: Students can use AI tools to identify real-world problems that require math to solve, allowing them to propose and develop their own projects.
3. Interactive Learning Paths: AI can provide various pathways through mathematical concepts, enabling students to choose their preferred mode: visual, auditory, or hands-on activities.

Science Class

1. Student-Designed Experiments: AI can assist students in designing their own experiments by suggesting variables and methods based on their interest, whether it is states of matter or life cycles.
2. Research Projects: AI can help students choose topics for research projects, supporting them with leveled resources and organizing their findings in creative ways.
3. Virtual Field Trips: AI can curate options for virtual field trips that align with student interests, allowing them to explore topics they are passionate about.

Social Studies Class

1. Cultural Research Projects: Students can choose a culture or community they are interested in and use AI tools to conduct research. They can explore aspects like traditions, languages, food, and social structures. AI can help students gather resources, suggest relevant articles, videos, and primary sources, and even help organize their research.
2. Interactive Timelines: Students can use AI to create interactive timelines that highlight key events in history, choosing events that interest them, adding multimedia elements.
3. Digital Storytelling: Students can create digital stories or documentaries on social issues, movements, or historical events using AI video-editing tools.
4. Virtual Discussions: AI chatbots can facilitate virtual discussions on various social studies topics. Students can engage with the chatbots to pose questions, define key terms, explore different perspectives, and receive prompts to encourage deeper thinking.

English Language Arts

1. Writing Prompts: AI can provide a range of writing prompts based on themes or genres, allowing students to select topics that resonate with them personally.
2. Reading Selections: Students and teachers can use AI to curate reading lists based on interests or themes they want to explore.

3. Interactive Vocabulary Builders: Using AI, students can create personalized vocabulary lists based on their reading materials. AI can generate quizzes, flashcards, and games to help reinforce learning and make vocabulary acquisition fun.

The Tool in Practice

We have deliberately chosen to be mainly platform-agnostic as the technology is changing and evolving so rapidly. Any examples we share may be obsolete tomorrow, so take each as illustrative, not prescriptive.

My sixth graders were working on a persuasive-writing task. I had decided it was a perfect opportunity to incorporate the use of AI to support them through the writing process. The students had all chosen a movie, book, or TV show they thought should be mandatory viewing or reading for every preteen. After students made their choice, they used AI to generate an outline for their persuasive writing. I taught my students how to refine their prompt to get their outline to match their own thinking. Once they had their outline, they shared it with me, and I let them know when they were ready to start writing. For the writing part, we discussed why it was important for this part of the process to not involve AI. I wanted my students, not AI, to develop these writing skills.

After they had drafted a text, we returned to AI. Students asked AI to give them feedback on their writing, particularly about how persuasive it was. The students conferred with me after they had received the feedback from AI, and we looked at it critically together.

I helped my students be critical users of feedback as we looked at specific suggestions and asked whether the feedback was valid or not. I also asked them if the feedback was important—did it address the criteria of the writing assignment? If not, we didn't spend too much time on it.

For students who finished their writing before the rest of the class, we also used AI to suggest extension activities, such as asking AI to generate some suggestions for real-world audiences for this persuasive writing.

Bootcamps

What Is It?

Bootcamp is a term we use for a self-contained introduction to a skill or a tool where students apply their learning immediately to a project with voice and choice in topic. Depending on the task design, there could also be choice in learner outcomes as well.

Why Do It? Peeling Back the Pedagogy

Bootcamps emphasize hands-on, active learning, allowing students to immediately apply new skills or knowledge to real-world projects. This approach enhances retention and understanding as students engage directly with the material. Working on projects in a condensed time frame enables teachers to provide immediate, constructive feedback. This iterative process helps students refine their skills and understand areas for improvement in real time. Bootcamps often encourage collaborative work, promoting peer interaction and knowledge sharing. This social aspect of learning helps students develop communication skills and learn from diverse perspectives. Because bootcamps are designed to build a specific skill set in a targeted manner, students can gain proficiency quickly, boosting their confidence in their abilities. The fast-paced nature of bootcamps encourages students to think critically and adapt to challenges as they arise, enhancing problem-solving abilities.

How to Do It

Some examples that we have used in our classes include:

- Google Workspace Bootcamp
- Canva Bootcamp
- Podcasting Bootcamp
- Online Exhibit/Website Bootcamp
- Creating an Infographic Bootcamp

1. **Define Objectives.**
   a. Skills Goals: Determine the specific skills or tools to be covered in the bootcamp.
   b. Learning Outcomes: Identify what students should be able to accomplish by the end relevant to the curriculum.
2. **Choose a Format.**
   a. Duration: Decide how long the bootcamp will run.
   b. Structure: Ensure that there is a mix of instruction, hands-on activities, and collaboration.
   c. Form: Provide clear criteria for the final project where students are applying what they have learned.
3. **Provide Resources and Support.**
   a. Guides and Tutorials: Offer reference materials, including written guides or video tutorials for self-paced learning.
   b. Teacher Support: Be actively present in the classroom offering support and suggestions on how to use the tools effectively.
4. **Showcase Learning (Optional).**
   a. Presentations: Conclude with a showcase where students present their final projects to the class or a wider audience.
   b. Certificates: Consider providing certificates or acknowledgments of completion to celebrate student achievements.

Consider incorporating an assessment loop that allows you to collect feedback on the bootcamp experience to inform future iterations and improvements.

The Tool in Practice

Google Workspace Bootcamp

In my seventh-grade classroom, the air buzzed with excitement as the students filed in for the week-long Google Tools Bootcamp. The challenge I'd set for them? To create a digital presentation exploring the impact of renewable energy on local communities.

On the first day, I introduced the students to Google Docs for research. I kicked things off with a quick demo, walking them through creating a Doc and the basics of writing and editing. As soon as I set them loose, Emma and Liam paired up and dove into articles about solar panels. I made my way around the room, offering tips on collaboration and helping with citation practices. Occasionally, I paused the class to highlight a feature in Google Docs that I knew would be helpful, a strategy of "just-in-time" teaching. It's such a great way to build their skills without overwhelming them all at once.

By midweek, we transitioned to Google Slides, and the creative energy in the room became electric. Each pair was deep into crafting their presentations, integrating visuals and data they'd compiled in Google Sheets. I overheard Liam say to Emma, "Let's use that chart from our research," as he pulled it seamlessly into their slides. I reminded the class about the short video tutorials I'd uploaded to Google Classroom. "Don't forget those if you're stuck—they'll walk you through everything we've learned this week," I said. It was rewarding to see students independently using those resources.

On Friday, the classroom transformed into a miniconference. Each pair presented their findings to the class, using Google Forms to gather peer feedback. Watching Emma and Liam's eyes light up as their peers praised their presentation was such a proud moment. One student wrote in the feedback form, "Your visuals really helped me understand what you were talking about." It was exactly the kind of thoughtful interaction I'd hoped for when planning the week.

As the final bell rang, I sat at my desk for a moment, reflecting on everything the students had accomplished. The bootcamp wasn't just about learning tech skills—it was about fostering teamwork, creativity, and deeper understanding. Watching my students take pride in their work and support one another reaffirmed why I love teaching. It was a week that left me feeling both inspired and grateful.

Podcasting Bootcamp

In my eighth-grade science class, students hurriedly took their seats for a Friday tradition—Bootcamp Day. I clapped my hands to get their attention and grinned. "Okay, everyone! Today, we're diving into a fun challenge: Create a thirty-second podcast to answer any one of the '100 Science Questions' you came up with at the beginning of the year."

The room buzzed with excitement as groups formed quickly. I noticed Amina, Raj, and Leila teaming up, their energy contagious. They grabbed laptops and iPads and started brainstorming. I caught snippets of their conversation as I walked by. "What is climate change?" Raj suggested, pointing to his list of questions. They jumped right in, researching greenhouse gasses and rising temperatures. "Let's keep it simple," Amina said, jotting down notes. "We need to explain why it matters!"

In one of our cozy recording corners, the trio huddled around a microphone. Raj took charge of the iPad and pressed Record. I paused nearby, listening as they spoke clearly and passionately. Leila's voice carried the explanation: "Climate change is the long-term alteration of temperature and typical weather patterns." She nailed the tone, emphasizing the urgency.

After a few takes—and plenty of laughs at their early stumbles—they were satisfied. I smiled as they played back their podcast, proud of their determination. "We nailed it!" Amina exclaimed, then scrambled to find their checklist, which had fallen to the floor. Leila grabbed it, and the team focused on their next steps: adding music and an introduction.

I stepped to the front of the room and called out, "For those of you who are ready for editing, the instructions are on the SMART Board. Tutorials are in your Google Classroom. If you need help, just call me over!"

As the final minutes ticked down, the classroom hummed with energy. There was a bit of a rush to turn in final recordings, but I didn't mind the frenzy. When the bell rang, I smiled, taking in the scene. My students hadn't just grasped the science—they'd learned how to communicate, collaborate, and create something they were proud of. Each group was excited to share their podcast, and I couldn't wait to listen to how they'd answered their burning science questions.

Checklists

What Is It?

Checklists are used to help students understand the components of a project or the steps needed to be successful in a given task. We use checklists to support students as they engage in personalized work, allowing them to work at their own pace. Checklists are also a way students can ensure they're meeting the criteria of a task.

Why Do It? Peeling Back the Pedagogy

When we give students the tools to manage their own workflows, their independence soars and ownership of the work also increases. Being able to work at their own pace while ensuring their work meets the criteria for an assignment allows students to feel confident in their ability to accomplish their goal.

Though checklists are a part of many teachers' regular practice, they are particularly helpful when offering students voice and choice as a method to support student independence when they're engaging in different kinds of work. For example, perhaps your class is learning about immigration to Western Canada in the 1800s and 1900s. You offer your students two options of ways to demonstrate their learning: an infographic or an advertisement. Checklists give your students a scaffold to support their independence when you have different students in the room doing different things at the same time.

How to Do It

Provide students with a checklist of the steps needed to accomplish a given task or project. Ensure the steps in the checklist align with the assessment criteria and support the students in meeting these criteria.

Supporting students in creating their own checklists for their projects is an advanced version of this protocol, and can even further increase student engagement and ownership in their work. This is a logical next step when supporting students in learning how to chunk their work into smaller components.

This protocol works very well with informal conferencing where students need to get the teacher's signature or initials before moving on. Building these teacher checkpoints into the process keeps students working independently but allows the teacher to mentor students on their next step and give them feedback as they work.

The Tool in Practice

Using the subject above, immigration to Western Canada, here are two sample checklists based on the choice of product students chose. You can see that both checklists focus on the same content, but give two different pathways to demonstrate understanding.

Creating an Infographic

Canada Immigration

Option 1: Infographic
- Complete each step.
- Have your teacher sign off before you continue.

Due: ____

❏ **Planning**   (sign off when complete) ____

Record 15-20 numbers (dates, populations, statistics, etc.) that relate to immigration to Western Canada in the late 1800s to early 1900s.

In your notebook, identify and explain how each number connects to (at least) one of the outcomes.

____

❏ **Creating**   (sign off when complete) ____

Open up Canva and search for a "graphic organizer" template that you like.

Create your infographic. Make sure you consider:
- ❏ Composition and placement: What is your focal point? Where does the eye go?
- ❏ Font, colour, and size: What fonts, font sizes, and font colors can you use to entice your viewer?
- ❏ Graphics and pictures: What images connect with your message?

❏ **Polishing**   (sign off when complete) ____

Edit your writing and refine your work to ensure you are ready to publish your work.
- ❏ Capitalize the first letter of the sentence and proper nouns like names, places, and events.
- ❏ Add end punctuation to your sentences.
- ❏ Read your work aloud to yourself or a partner to catch fluency issues.
- ❏ Run a spell check and grammar check on your work.

Creating an Advertisement

Canada Immigration

Option 2: Advertisement
- Complete each step.
- Have your teacher sign off before you continue.

Due: ____

❏ **Planning**   (sign off when complete) ______________________________________

Convince someone to immigrate to Western Canada from (choose one):
- ❏ Europe
- ❏ Eastern Canada
- ❏ Ukraine
- ❏ United States
- ❏ Asia

Push factors are reasons for a person to leave a place. Pull factors are reasons for a person to come to a place.
- ❏ Identify the push factors of someone from that place who might move to Western Canada. Jot your ideas down in your notebook or in a document.
- ❏ Identify the pull factors for someone who might want to move to Western Canada. Jot your ideas down in your notebook or in a document.
- ❏ Use your textbook, reference materials, and the web to support your ideas.

In your notebook, brainstorm possibilities for each persuasive technique.
- ❏ Pathos: Appealing to someone's emotions. Tug at their heartstrings and make them feel positive about immigrating.
- ❏ Logos: Appealing to logic and reason. Use logic and reason to convince someone to come. Include statistics and evidence.
- ❏ Ethos: Appealing to credibility or reliability. Use a reliable person or expert to lend their expertise to your campaign.

❏ **Creating**   (sign off when complete) ______________________________________

Open up Canva and use a blank template or find an advertisement or flyer template you want to work from.

Create your advertisement. Make sure you consider:
- ❏ Composition and placement: What is your focal point? Where does the eye go?
- ❏ Font, color, and size: What fonts, font sizes, and font colors can you use to entice your viewer?
- ❏ Graphics and pictures: What images connect with your message?

❏ **Polishing**   (sign off when complete) ______________________________________

Edit your writing and refine your work to ensure you are ready to publish your work.
- ❏ Capitalize the first letter of the sentence and proper nouns like names, places, and events.
- ❏ Add end punctuation to your sentences.
- ❏ Read your work aloud to yourself or a partner to catch fluency issues.
- ❏ Run a spell check and grammar check on your work.

Decision Paralysis Tools

What Is It?

When students are given voice and choice in their learning, especially if this is not something they are used to, it can sometimes be challenging to make a decision. Students can be paralyzed by so many great ideas and too many options. Sometimes they need strategies and tools to get them out of this state of decision paralysis.

Why Do It? Peeling Back the Pedagogy

These tools support students in deciding between different possibilities. Usually a tool like this would be employed on a one-on-one basis when a student needs it, but it can sometimes be used by a whole class to make a decision.

How to Do It

Enabling Constraints

Coined by Erin Manning and Brian Massumi, an enabling constraint is the application of a rule in order to encourage creativity. You will be familiar with enabling constraints if you've ever seen cooking shows like *Iron Chef* or *Chopped*. The rules of these shows are that the chef must use and highlight the secret ingredient in the dish she makes. The addition of a constraint focuses the creator on a defined goal, enabling creativity to flourish in the execution of this goal.

In a classroom setting, enabling constraints depend on what task your students are completing. Here are some ideas for enabling constraints:

- Format/Mode: Rhyme scheme in poetry, format of poetry (haiku, limerick, sonnet, etc.), text message, advertisement, podcast, video, short story, comic, artwork, T-shirt design, shoe design, etc.
- Genre: Dystopian, realistic, fairy tale, suspense, thriller, horror, mystery, etc.
- Size: The project must fit in this box, it must be miniature, it must be oversized, etc.
- Number: It must contain three _______, identify ten uses of ________, etc.
- Topic: It must be about________.
- Time: You have _____ minutes/hours/days/weeks to complete the work.
- People: Set a descriptor to support group formation. For example, you have to work with someone you haven't before.

In order to encourage creativity, the other aspects of the assignment must involve choice. For instance, if the topic is predetermined by you as a constraint, then the students should be able to choose how they communicate their understanding of this topic.

Gamification

There are many different game mechanics that can support decision-making when a student is stuck. Here are a few of them:

- Flip a Coin: Assign Option A to Heads and Option B to Tails. Flip a coin and pursue whichever option is revealed.
- Roll a Die: This is essentially the flip-a-coin method but with six different options instead of two.

- Action Cards: Create cards that reveal different options or ideas to incorporate into the work. For example, a teacher could use cards in narrative writing. Cards could be different characters to incorporate, different conflicts to add, objects to incorporate, vocabulary words, etc.

Gut Check

Gut Check, a method borrowed from the *Field Guide to Human Centred Design* (IDEO, 2015), is exactly what it sounds like: looking at all the options and checking in with your heart, your head, and your gut to decide which option is most promising. In the context of students engaging in project work in the classroom, you can invite students to do a gut check when struggling with a decision. Asking simple questions such as, "Which option feels right to you?" or "What would be most interesting and engaging for you?" students can check in with themselves to make a decision.

A gut check can also be a good tool to use after using another method such as flipping a coin. After the coin reveals the option, invite students to check to see if the answer the coin revealed feels right to them.

The Tool in Practice

In my grade five English language arts classroom, we were diving into narrative writing, and many of my students were struggling with how to move their stories forward. That day, I introduced a twist: Action Cards. I explained the activity as I held up a deck of colorful cards.

"Each of these has an idea to help you stretch your story. It might be a character, a conflict, an object, or even a vocabulary word. You'll draw a card and find a way to incorporate it into your story. If you get stuck while you're writing and aren't sure where to go next, you can come and draw another card."

There was a lot of excitement and some nervous murmurs.

"Does this mean I have to rewrite my whole story if it doesn't fit?" Zara asked.

"Not at all," I replied. "Think of it as a way to add something new. Maybe it deepens your conflict or gives your character a challenge to overcome. It's about being creative and flexible, and making decisions."

I shuffled the deck and started circulating around the room. Mohammad was the first to draw. He grinned when he read his card: *An unexpected storm.* His story was about two siblings on a camping trip, and I could already see the wheels turning.

"I didn't know how to make my story exciting, but now… maybe the storm traps them in the tent," he mused, "or maybe it washes away their supplies."

"That's a great direction, Mohammad. Think about how this could push your characters to grow," I encouraged.

At another table, Aya drew *A mysterious key.* Her eyes widened, and she flipped to a scene where her main character was sneaking through an old library.

"The key could be hidden in one of the books!" she exclaimed. "But what does it open?"

"Great question," I answered. "You're building suspense—just make sure to answer your question later."

Some students, like Ian, struggled at first. His card said *A new character enters,* and he wasn't sure how to introduce someone into his medieval fantasy story.

"Why not think about who could make things harder, or easier, for your hero?" I suggested. I could see he had an idea, and he immediately started sketching out the details for a rogue knight who would betray the hero.

By the end of class, their stories had all taken unexpected and creative turns. The Action Cards had pushed them out of their comfort zones. The design constraint had helped them dig into richer, more dynamic storytelling and had taken away their sense of being overwhelmed by too many possibilities. I was curious to see if anyone would choose to draw another card the next day.

Flat Sheets

What Is It?

Flat sheets are a teacher-created tool that can significantly facilitate the incorporation of voice and choice in your classroom. They are student guides to support independent work such as how to create a picture book, how to annotate a novel, song, or video, how to record a podcast, or what the elements of a good review are. Flat sheets help students understand expectations for an assignment and recognize what excellence looks like. They can be anchor charts, posters, individual handouts, or even bookmarks. When flat sheets are done well, students are able to use them to support independence. This allows for a greater variety of choices in the classroom. You will notice we also reference this tool in use as part of other tools because of its versatility.

Why Do It? Peeling Back the Pedagogy

Flat sheets provide students with a clear outline of assignment expectations and criteria for success. This transparency helps reduce anxiety and confusion, which promotes independence in the student. Flat sheets can be step-by-step guides or even checklists. As reference tools, they reinforce learning and aid in the retention of information. By using flat sheets across different assignments, teachers can create a consistent framework for students. This consistency helps students develop familiarity with expectations. A flat sheet should present information visually and textually, helping all students to understand the concepts.

How to Do It

1. Define the Purpose: Clearly outline the specific goal of the flat sheet, whether it's to guide students on a project, explain a key concept, or outline expectations.
2. Know Your Audience: Consider the diverse needs of your students, including varying levels of ability, learning styles, and cultural backgrounds. Tailor the language, visuals, and complexity of the content accordingly. You can also easily differentiate this resource for your students.
3. Organize Information Clearly: Use headings, bullet points, and numbered lists to break down information into digestible sections. A logical flow helps students easily follow the steps or concepts being presented.
4. Use Visuals: Incorporate relevant images, diagrams, or icons to support the text. Visuals can enhance understanding and make the flat sheet more engaging.
5. Incorporate Examples: Provide concrete examples to illustrate key concepts.
6. Include Checklists or Criteria: This helps students self-assess and understand their next steps.

7. Make It Accessible: Ensure the flat sheet is easy to read, using legible fonts, appropriate color contrasts, and clear layouts. This is a great opportunity to model the type of work and considerations you expect from students.
8. Encourage Reflection: Including prompts for self-reflection or questions that encourage students to think about their learning process reinforces metacognition skills.

Don't forget to invite students to offer suggestions and improvements for clarity and effectiveness. Use this feedback to iterate future versions and to model the growth process you expect students to embrace.

The Tool in Practice

In my sixth-grade class, I had set the stage for a day of independent math exploration. On the board, I had written: *"Today's Challenge: Create Your Own Math Game!"*

As the students settled into groups, I handed out flat sheets with guidelines on game creation, examples, and a checklist for success. The sheets included diagrams illustrating key concepts like probability and geometry, and the success checklist that was also displayed on the SMART Board. I spent a few minutes reviewing the criteria with the whole class before they got to work.

In one corner, Aisha, Omar, and Priya flipped through their sheets.

"Let's make a board game using fractions," Aisha suggested, her eyes lighting up.

Omar nodded, pulling out a sketchpad. "We can use the checklist to make sure we include all the rules!"

Across the room, Javier and Mei brainstormed ideas for a card game based on multiplication. They referred to their flat sheets to check the elements of a good game, making sure they incorporated teamwork and strategy.

As the class worked, I wandered around, offering guidance. Students frequently consulted their sheets, using them as roadmaps for their projects. One group struggled to reach a consensus, as each member wanted their idea to be the group's idea. I spent several minutes supporting their negotiations so they could move forward.

At the end of class, each group pitched their game, showcasing their creativity and the math concepts they had incorporated. The next day, the class used heat mapping to vote for their top six games. These games were to be further developed, built, and then added to the library collection, where other classes could check them out and play. I smiled as I watched my students thrive, each flat sheet having guided them toward independence and success in their math journey.

Here's an example of a set of instructions for designing a board game.

Create a Board Game: Cells & Systems Edition

Your Guide to Designing, Creating, and Testing a Science-Based Game

What Your Game Must Include

A theme and clear goal (e.g., escape the infection, system shutdown)
At least 4 human body systems and how they work together
Accurate use of key science terms
Cards, tokens, dice, or other pieces that fit your theme
Rules, instructions, and a clear way to win

Remember to use YOUR ideas—remix and reimagine, but don't copy another game!

Science Check: Key Ideas to Include

Include facts and vocabulary from these topics in your cards, game actions, or board design:

Cell Theory

Microscopes and Cells

Cell Parts and Their Jobs

Body Systems

System Interaction

Healthy vs. Disrupted System Function

Example: A "System Breakdown" card might say: "You're low on oxygen! Your respiratory and circulatory systems are failing. Miss a turn while your team recovers."

Elements of a Good Game

Clear Goal Players know what they are trying to do (for example: collect all body systems, survive an outbreak, restore system function).	**Easy to Learn** Instructions and rules are simple and clear. New players can understand how to play quickly.	**Fair and Balanced** Every player has a fair chance. No one starts with an advantage, and the rules apply to everyone.
Interesting Choices Players have to make decisions, not just follow the same steps every time. Strategy and thinking matter.	**Science Is Everywhere** Science facts are built into the way the game works—not just on trivia cards. You use science ideas to play and win.	**Visually Organized** The board and pieces are neat, easy to read, and labeled clearly. The design helps players understand what's happening.
Replay Value People can play more than once and still enjoy it. Different choices or strategies can lead to different outcomes.		

Create a Board Game: Cells & Systems Edition (cont'd)

Game Mechanics: How Will Your Game Work?

You can choose one or more mechanics to build your game around:

Mechanic	What It Means	Example
Action Selection	Players choose actions each turn.	"Draw a card" or "Heal a body part"
Tile Placement	Build the board as you go.	Place system tiles to create full body systems.
Deck Building	Collect helpful cards.	Build a hand of organ cards to stay healthy.
Worker Placement	Send tokens to do tasks.	Place a nurse on the "oxygen refill" station.
Trivia/Challenge Cards	Answer questions to move forward.	"What organ filters blood?"
Race to the End	First to complete the task wins.	"Fix all your body systems before time runs out!"

Plan → Build → Playtest → Revise → Reflect

Plan	Choose theme, mechanics, and group roles.
Build	Create board, pieces, cards, and rules.
Playtest	Play your game with another group and get feedback.
Revise	Make improvements based on feedback.
Reflect	Complete your group and personal reflection.

Final Self-Check: Is Your Science Clear?

❏ We included at least 4 human body systems.
❏ We explained how those systems interact.
❏ We used accurate vocabulary (e.g., organ names, cell parts, system functions).
❏ Our cards, board, or game elements show correct information.
❏ We communicated our ideas in a way that others can understand and learn from.

Remember: Your game doesn't have to look fancy—what matters is that it helps players understand cells and systems accurately.

Idea Generators

What Is It?

Idea generators can be great tools to use to come up with possibilities for students to pursue in creative projects. Idea generators give students a structure to come up with ideas. In using the tools, they may find that they push their ideas further creatively than they might otherwise.

Why Do It? Peeling Back the Pedagogy

Students who are inexperienced in creativity often want to choose one of the first few ideas they have. When offering students voice and choice, we want to ensure that the work they do is worth doing. Otherwise, what's the point? The purpose of offering students voice and choice in their work is to augment engagement and make school a place of liberation and joy. Generating their own ideas is one way students can come up with ideas they are interested in and care about.

How to Do It

There are several different idea generators out there. Here are a few of our favorites.

SCAMPER

One brainstorming strategy you may be familiar with is called SCAMPER, which stands for Substitute, Combine, Adapt, Modify, Put to Another Use, Eliminate, and Reverse. SCAMPER The Fast Idea Generator tool can be found in DIY's Development Impact and You toolkit. It is a ready-to-use template to use for SCAMPER-style brainstorming. The SCAMPER technique was developed by Alex Osborne in the 1930s, and later refined by Bob Eberle in the 1970s (SCAMPER, n.d.). Designed for business development but easily adapted for use with kids, it can be obtained freely online by visiting https://diy-toolkit.org/tools/fast-idea-generator/

This tool gives participants prompts that help them reimagine an idea to see how far they could push it. We will show you exactly how this brainstorming strategy can offer many exciting options in "The Tool in Practice" below, where we will ask it to help a student brainstorm how he might show that LeBron James is the "Greatest of All Time" (GOAT) basketball player.

AI Idea Generators

AI tools can offer great ideas when starting with an option or an idea. Most AI tools will work to help generate ideas, such as ChatGPT or Google Gemini, but there are also more specific tools related to idea generation, such as https://www.getvoila.ai/ai-tools/idea-generator. Remember our earlier caveat about the obsolescence of tech tools.

We asked several different AI idea generators to give us ideas for projects a grade-five student could create to show that LeBron James is the GOAT, and we got many creative suggestions, our favorite being to design a basketball card collection highlighting LeBron James's career accomplishments.

Reversed Brainstorming

Reversed brainstorming (Elmansy, 2024) is an unexpected and fun process that asks participants to share their *worst* ideas first before attempting to find the best solutions. Participants begin with the problem or question they want to solve. In our example, our question is, "How can I show that LeBron James is the GOAT?"

The next step involves asking what the *worst* answers to the question might be. In this step, a student might suggest the worst ways to show LeBron James's genius are to make a coloring book with pictures of LeBron, deliver a boring, hour-long speech about every fact ever recorded about LeBron, or create a book that shares many famous basketball players' paths to success *except* LeBron's. None of these ideas answer the student's question. The coloring book does nothing to address LeBron's success, the speech aims to bore rather than to inspire, and the book doesn't address LeBron at all. The next step is to reverse these ideas again, flipping them from the *worst* ideas to the *best* ideas. My student might flip these ideas as such: Design a coloring book that includes statistics and facts integrated into the visuals showing LeBron's accomplishments; deliver a short, motivating speech about how LeBron is inspiring and someone we should all look up to; and create a book comparing several different basketball stars, including LeBron, showing how LeBron is objectively the GOAT.

The Tool in Practice

Declan was obsessed with basketball. Every day, he came into school, removed his outdoor sneakers, and carefully put on his shockingly white Nike Jordans. He walked gingerly down the hall so as not to crease his shoes. He opened his locker, which was plastered with pages torn from magazines—images of Kobe Bryant, Steph Curry, Michael Jordan, Victor Wembanyama, and his favorite, LeBron James. He endured his morning classes, looking forward to lunch. His entire lunch hour was spent on one of the school's courts—outdoors if it was nice out, or in the gym if it was open for the grade sevens to use at lunch. He wolfed down his sandwich quickly so he could get out there and play as soon as possible.

Declan was, shall we say, decidedly *not* obsessed with language arts. For the entire month of September, he sighed whenever I asked the class to take out their independent reading books—the way we began every class. Reading was boring to him. He wasn't interested in novels or characters he couldn't imagine. As I got to know Declan better and learned about his love of basketball, I knew I could hook him into reading and writing if I used his passion to get him there.

In October, I slipped a book into his hands at the beginning of independent reading: *Basketball's Greatest Stars*. His eyes widened, and he started turning the pages quickly to get past the book's front matter. He devoured that book. The sighs stopped almost immediately. I even caught him reading it under his desk when he was supposed to be working on something else.

After my students had some time to get into their independent reading books, I asked them to create a project that would show their understanding of what they'd read. I left it wide open: *Design a project you are excited to complete that shows your takeaways from your independent reading book.*

As the students worked on brainstorming their ideas, I noticed Declan's head down on the desk.

"What's up, bud?" I asked.

"Hmmm. I don't know what to do for my project. I think I want to do something about LeBron, but I don't know what to do," he mumbled into the desk. He lifted his head. "All I can think of is like a podcast or something, but that sounds boring."

"Ah, well. Let's try a brainstorming tool to get you going. I know you loved that book and you love LeBron, so it should be easy to come up with some ideas. Let's start with your podcast idea, and we'll go from there." I pulled up a chair to sit with him at his desk and put a blank copy of the Fast Idea Generator in front of him. "Let's do it together."

We talked our way through the graphic organizer, coming up with some interesting options.

"Okay, this actually sounds really fun. And it's okay if I get Dante, Jesse, and Kaiden to help me?" he asked, naming a few of his friends from the basketball team.

"Yes, of course. As long as they get their projects done too," I said. "So, you should start by working on a script for the intro, the questions you're going to ask, and think about music and production."

Declan walked to the laptop cart and got out his laptop, walking carefully, of course, so he didn't crease his shoes.

Fast Idea Generator

The idea I'm starting from is: *A 15-minute podcast about the genius of LeBron James*	
Substitute What can we replace?	*I'm going to substitute my idea of a podcast with an interactive exhibit for a museum about LeBron's genius.*
Combine What features or parts can we combine?	*I'm going to combine video and audio and make this a YouTube video podcast.*
Adapt What can we tweak or adjust?	*I'm going to adapt the podcast format into a sports documentary-style series with expert panels, similar to ESPN's 30 for 30. It will be a 12-part series called "Who's the GOAT?" where the experts debate who the GOAT is in a variety of different sports. The panel of invited experts will offer their nominee for the GOAT in that sport and then the guests will debate.*
Modify What can we minimize? What can we maximize?	*I'm going to make an encyclopedia about LeBron, collecting together every single statistic and compiling everything that's ever been written about him. Or, I'm going to shrink it down to a single TikTok video splicing together LeBron's best shots.*
Put to Another Use What can we learn from a different field?	*I'm going to learn from the field of amusement parks and make a Lebron amusement park.*
Eliminate What can we get rid of or simplify?	*I'm going to eliminate some of the length of a traditional podcast and condense it down into a 5-minute podcast.*

What idea have you ended up with? Which of your ideas is most promising?

I really love the idea of the GOAT series. I won't have time to do a 12-part series, but reimagining my podcast as a debate podcast is really exciting. I'll record the basketball episode, and I'll invite some of my friends to join me as guests, with one of them arguing LeBron is the GOAT, one arguing for Michael Jordan, one arguing Kobe Bryant, and one arguing Steph Curry. I'll ask the questions and moderate the discussion, and then make the decision at the end about which player is the GOAT.

Kanban Board

What Is It?

A kanban board is a tool that is attributed to Toyota. In Japanese, "kanban" means "visual sign," and it was created by the Japanese car manufacturer to manage work related to a specific project (Hennigan and Botteroff, 2024). When a team is working together on a large project, they work to identify all the parts of the project and then sort them into columns on a visual board. Often kanban boards include columns such as "To Do," "In Progress," and "Done." They can also include optional categories such as "Under Review." Tasks that are a part of the project are then written on cards or sticky notes. Everything begins in the "To Do" column, but then as people begin to work on each component, the cards get moved through to the "In Progress," and "Done" columns. Names of group members responsible for each component can be attached to the card as it is moved to the "In Progress" column, which helps to ensure every group member is actively contributing to the group's goal.

Why Do It? Peeling Back the Pedagogy

When working on complex and collaborative projects, students need scaffolds to manage the work and the workload. A kanban board supports both of these goals. When the parts of a project can be made into tangible, moveable parts, a large, complex task becomes manageable. Everyone working on the task can see what parts are being worked on and what parts still need to be done. In fact, we used a version of a kanban board when writing this book so we could see what needed to be done and which one of us was doing which parts as we wrote asynchronously in our own homes.

Every teacher knows that collaboration can be challenging, as we want to ensure all students are contributing to the task and engaging in the learning. A kanban board ensures every student takes responsibility for a part of the project, and we can easily see which student was responsible for which parts of the work.

How to Do It

1. Set up an area for each group's kanban board. Chart paper works well, but you'll need wall space to display the kanban boards. You'll want to ensure two things when you place them:
   a. They should be spread out from each other so groups can interact with them easily.
   b. They should be constantly visible to serve as a visual reminder of what is being done and what still needs doing. While it may be tempting to utilize hallway real estate so the boards can be spread out, it's not advisable as then they are not in the work environment of the students while they are doing the work. Alternatively, kanban boards can be rolled up and then placed on desks or tables during work sessions.
2. Divide the kanban board into three parts: "To Do," "In Progress," and "Done." You may also add "Under Review" after "In Progress" if you want to build in a peer feedback loop for the group.
3. Engage each group in identifying the components of the task. See the "Time Management Strategies" protocol: The "chunking" strategy works well here. Have students write the components on index cards or sticky notes. Place these cards or notes in the "To Do" column.

4. Explain to students that they now need to move the components through the "In Progress" column to the "Done" column. Each student will select one of the components to take responsibility for, and move into the "In Progress" column. A conversation about prioritizing might fit this discussion, as there may be certain components that must be done before others. Have the students write their name on the card they are moving to the "In Progress" column.

5. The next step is to get to work! Students work on their component, and when they are finished, they move the card to the "Done" column. If you are adding the step of "Under Review," each student should choose another peer's card and write their name on it as "Reviewer." This student's job is to review the work their fellow group member did and give feedback for improvement before moving to the "Done" column.

6. Once the card has been moved to the "Done" column, the student returns to the "To Do" column, chooses another card, and then repeats the process until all the cards have been moved to "Done."

The Tool in Practice

My students had formed groups to carry out kindness campaigns around the school in honor of Pink Shirt Day, a national day to end bullying. Each group had brainstormed different ideas for kindness projects and had decided on unique ways to spread kindness around the school.

"Okay, friends, it's time to get into your groups. You'll see that I have created kanban boards for you, which are posted on the walls around the room. There's one for each group. Can you go sit by your kanban board now?" I gave the students a few moments to get settled, then explained a bit about the history of the kanban board and how it worked.

"So your first step is to identify all the parts of your project. I want you to use the sticky notes and Sharpies I put on your tables and write each of the parts on a different sticky note," I explained.

I circulated while a buzz of energetic talking filled the room as the groups thought aloud about what needed to be done.

One group wanted to set up a buddy bench at recess for kids who needed a friend to play with.

"Oh, and then we need to talk to the principal to get permission," Gemma said. "If we want to put a sign on it. Or maybe we would even be allowed to paint the bench. It's pretty old and chipping anyway. Maybe we would be allowed! No harm in asking."

"Yeah, and then create the sign!" added Fernando.

"We should probably do some kind of advertising to let kids know about it? Maybe we could visit every classroom to let them know about it? And maybe put it on the announcements too. So we'd need to write a script for that," Rory suggested. Gemma wrote both steps down on a sticky note.

After the groups had enough time to identify the parts of their projects, I invited them to place their sticky notes on their group's board in the "To Do" column, sorted chronologically. Which tasks needed to be done first? Which ones last?

"Okay, and now we get to work! I want each of you to choose one of the tasks at the top of your column and write your name on the sticky note. Move it into the 'In Progress' column, and then you will get started! There might be some tasks that more than one of you needs to help with, but your name on the sticky note means you are the person responsible for completing this task. Your goal is to move your stickies to the 'Done' column. Once all your stickies have been moved to 'Done,' you can be confident that you've completed your project!"

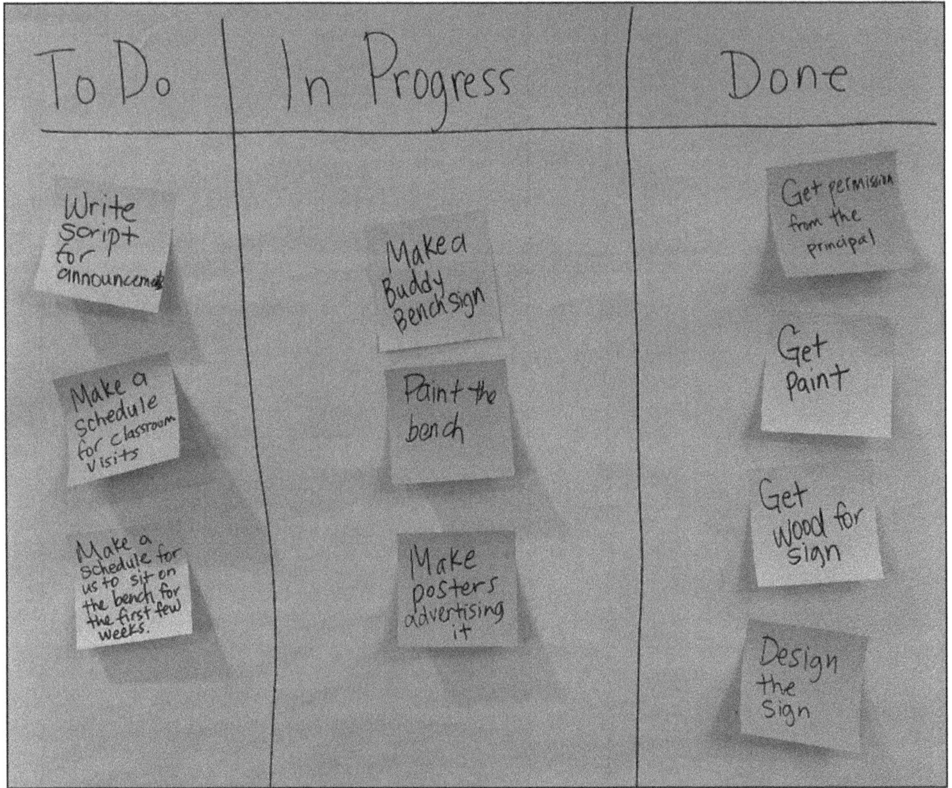

Peer Feedback Frameworks

What Is It?

Peer feedback frameworks are structured approaches that allow students to provide constructive feedback to their peers. They are designed to support learning by encouraging students to engage critically with each other's work, reflect on their own understandings and develop key skills of communication, collaboration, and critical thinking.

Why Do It? Peeling Back the Pedagogy

Peer feedback, when done in a psychologically safe environment with clear expectations and guidelines, can lead to significant improvements in learning outcomes. Van Gennip, Segers, and Tillema (2009) found that peer feedback can positively influence students' self-regulation and engagement. Students who participate in peer feedback are more likely to take responsibility for their own learning and show increased motivation to improve. It promotes deeper learning as students engage more critically with the material when evaluating their peers' work (Topping, 1998). The work of Hattie and Timperley (2007) highlighted that feedback can have a substantial impact on learning when it is specific and timely and involves active student engagement. The iterative process of giving and receiving feedback helps students refine their understanding and produces higher-quality outcomes when the students are given time to implement the feedback.

Choice is particularly relevant in having students ask for what they want feedback on, what feedback they are going to accept, and how they are going to act on that feedback. Student engagement can be increased through peer feedback because it actively engages students in the learning process. Students are more likely to take responsibility for their own learning and show increased motivation to improve (Falchikov, 1998). This is underpinned by Vygotsky's social constructivist theory which suggests that peer feedback facilitates collaborative learning, where students construct knowledge together, leading to deeper understanding. This interaction not only improves academic skills but also enhances social and communication skills.

It should also be noted that peer feedback can play a vital role in preparing students for life beyond school. The ability to give and receive feedback is essential in many workplaces, and practicing these skills help students build competencies they will need going forward.

How to Do It

When implementing peer feedback you will want to take into account the following considerations:

- Clear Guidelines: Ensure that you are providing clear instructions and expectations for the feedback so that students can be supportive.
- Modeling: Demonstrate how to give and receive effective feedback.
- Practice: The more opportunities your students have to practice giving feedback the better they will become at this process.
- Reflection: Provide opportunity for students to use and apply the feedback they receive to improve their work.

Peer feedback is most successful in a classroom where constructive criticism is valued and respected. Students need to feel safe giving and receiving feedback. This can be supported through clear understanding of the objectives and criteria so that students are able to give quality feedback that has value.

Here are some common peer feedback frameworks:

1. **Ladder of Feedback**
   - Clarify: Ask questions to clarify anything that is unclear.
   - Value: Highlight strengths and what you value about the work.
   - Concerns: What concerns do you have or what areas could be improved?
   - Suggestions: Offer specific suggestions for improvement.
2. **TAG Feedback**
   - Tell something you like about the work.
   - Ask a question to clarify or prompt further thinking.
   - Give a specific suggestion for improvement.
3. **Two Stars and a Wish**
   - Two Stars: The feedback giver identifies two positive aspects of the work.
   - One Wish: They suggest one area for improvement.
4. **Praise — Question — Polish (PQP)**
   - Praise: Highlight what is well done.

- **Question:** Pose questions that prompt deeper thinking or ask for clarification.
   - **Polish:** Offer constructive criticism or suggestions for refinement.
5. **Critique Protocol**
   - Warm Fuzzy Feedback: Begin with specific positive comments.
   - Cool Prickly Feedback: Provide constructive criticism.
   - Actionable Feedback: Suggest specific, actionable steps for improvement.
6. **Peer Review Sheets**
   - Students use the assessment rubric to evaluate each other's work against the set criteria.
   - This can be incorporated into a form or worksheet that includes the elements of the rubric, specific questions, or prompts.
7. **360-Degree Feedback**
   - Students receive feedback from multiple peers, each focusing on a different aspect of the work.
8. **Stop, Start, Continue Framework**
   - Stop: Suggest something that the student should stop doing because it is not effective.
   - Start: Recommend something new they could start doing to improve their work.
   - Continue: Point out something the student is doing well and should continue doing.
9. **Gallery Walks**
   - Work is displayed around the classroom and students rotate to provide feedback.
   - This allows for multiple rounds of feedback and is more dynamic and interactive.
   - It can, however, be more difficult to monitor the feedback.
10. **Glows and Grows**
    - Glows: Highlight what "glows" in the work — what shines or stands out positively.
    - Grows: Identify any areas where the student can "grow" or improve.

One of the most powerful applications of AI in the classroom is in providing detailed, constructive feedback. Traditional feedback often comes at the end of an assignment or it lacks specificity. AI can facilitate ongoing feedback throughout the learning process. This immediate and tailored feedback allows students to identify areas for growth and make improvements in real time. For example:

1. Real-Time Feedback: AI tools can analyze student work instantly, providing immediate feedback on assignments and projects. This allows students to understand mistakes and correct them before final submissions.
2. Personalized Suggestions: AI can generate tailored suggestions based on individual needs for improvement, suggesting targeted exercises to strengthen skills.
3. Progress Tracking: AI can support kids in tracking progress over time, helping students and teachers to set personalized goals and monitor improvements.
4. Interactive Feedback: Chatbots can provide interactive feedback, allowing students to ask questions and receive guidance as they work.

5. Multimodal Feedback: AI can provide feedback in various formats — text, audio, or visual — catering to different learning preferences and needs.

The Tool in Practice

Ladder of Feedback

In my grade-nine science class, we were wrapping up our lab reports on chemical reactions. I decided to have the students practice giving peer feedback in pairs using the Ladder of Feedback framework. I explained the process at the start of the lesson.

"Okay, everyone, here's how this works," I said. "You'll give feedback to your partner in four steps: Clarify, Value, Concerns, and Suggestions. Start by asking questions to clarify anything that's unclear. Then, highlight what you value in their work. Next, share any concerns—constructively! Finally, offer suggestions for improvement. Let's aim for kindness and specifics, yeah?"

The students nodded, some more enthusiastically than others. I paired Khadija with Liam and Arjun with Maria.

As I walked around, I overheard Khadija speaking with Liam.

"So, Liam," she said, glancing at his lab report. "You wrote that the reaction was 'vigorous,' but I'm not sure what you mean. Like, were there bubbles? Was it loud? Can you clarify that?"

Liam scratched his head. "Oh, right. Yeah, there were a lot of bubbles and a sizzling sound. I guess I didn't describe that very well. Thanks. I'll fix it."

Khadija nodded. "Okay, cool. I also think your hypothesis is strong—it makes sense and connects to the experiment really well. I like that."

"Thanks!" Liam said, smiling a bit.

"But," she added, flipping to the conclusion, "I think you can explain more about why the reaction happened the way it did. You wrote about what happened but not why."

"Ah, yeah, I wasn't sure how much detail to add there," Liam admitted.

Khadija thought for a moment. "Maybe you could include something about the reactants and how they combine—like the transfer of energy? That might make it clearer."

"Good idea," he said, jotting down notes.

By the end of the activity, I could see students leaning in, pointing at papers, and genuinely listening to each other. As the class wrapped up, I asked, "How did that feel?"

"Helpful," Maria said. "It's easier to improve when someone's specific."

Arjun chimed in, "Yeah, and I don't feel like a jerk when we start by saying something good."

I smiled. "Exactly. You've all got great ideas—you just need to share them the right way."

Two Stars and a Wish

In our grade-five social studies class, we had just finished a project about Canadian regions. Students had created posters showcasing their chosen region's geography, resources, and culture. That day, we were practicing peer feedback in pairs using Two Stars and a Wish.

"Alright, class," I began, standing at the front with the protocol on the SMART Board. "When you give feedback, find two stars—that's two things you really like or think were done well. Then share one wish, which is something that could make the work even better. Remember to be kind, helpful, and specific."

The students nodded, and I could see a mix of excitement and nerves. They paired up with their elbow partners. As they got started, I circulated around the room, tuning in to their conversations.

Jazmin was studying Eli's poster about the Rocky Mountains.

"Okay, so my first star is your pictures. The photos of the mountains and lakes are awesome—they really stand out," Jazmin enthused, pointing to the neatly printed images. "And my second star is the way you explained the resources. I didn't know they mined so much coal there."

"Thanks!" Eli replied, grinning.

"But for my wish," Jazmin continued, "I think you could add more about the Indigenous peoples in the area. Like, maybe include how they use the land?"

Eli nodded. "Yeah, I wasn't sure where to put that, but I can add it near the resources section."

Meanwhile, Neha was giving Aaron feedback on his poster about the Prairies.

"I really like how you showed the crops with pictures and charts. That's my first star," Neha began. "And my second star is your handwriting—it's super clear. I could read everything right away."

Aaron laughed. "Thanks. My mom made me rewrite it twice."

Neha smiled. "For my wish, maybe you could explain more about the weather? Like, why it's so dry there."

Aaron nodded thoughtfully. "Good idea. I'll add that."

By the end of the activity, the students had swapped papers and given feedback to a second peer.

"So how did it go?" I asked the class as we wrapped up.

"It was kind of fun," Aaron admitted. "I liked hearing what people thought I did well."

"And the wishes weren't mean," Jazmin added. "It's like getting ideas to make your work better."

"Exactly," I said. "Feedback is about helping each other grow—and you all did a great job with that today."

Gallery Walk

In my grade six math class, students had worked hard creating posters featuring multi-step math word problems with real-world connections. That day, we were using a Gallery Walk for peer feedback. I handed each student five sticky notes and set clear expectations.

"Here's the plan," I stated. "You'll rotate around the room and give feedback to five different people. Write one sticky note per poster. Include your name at the bottom so I know who wrote it. Remember: Be specific, kind, and helpful. Use point form, like this:

> *Something that works well*
> *Something that could be clearer or improved*

To monitor the feedback process, I moved around the room as students began, reading over their shoulders and stepping in to guide where needed.

At Aisha's poster, Jaden hesitated with his sticky note. He started to write: *"Confusing."*

"Jaden," I suggested, crouching next to him, "think about what's unclear. Is it the problem, the explanation, or the math steps?"

He nodded and rewrote:

Meanwhile, Priya carefully added feedback to Mateo's poster:

To help everyone stay accountable, I paused halfway through. "Quick check-in!" I announced. "Before you stick your notes, reread them. Does your feedback answer one of the prompts? Is it clear enough for your classmate to act on?"

At the end of the Gallery Walk, students retrieved the sticky notes from their posters and reflected on the feedback.

Aisha shared, "Jaden helped me catch a math error I hadn't noticed."

Mateo said, "Priya's question made me think about my explanation. I'm going to add a sentence to make it clearer."

The sticky notes not only made feedback manageable but also gave me a way to spot-check comments as they worked. By tying names to feedback, students stayed thoughtful and accountable, and I could step in when needed.

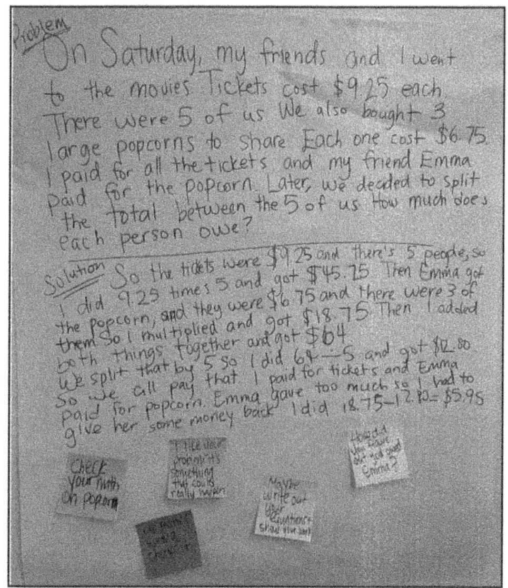

Sample student feedback

AI Feedback

In this scenario, based on actual in-class work, the specific examples were created with AI support.

In my grade-eight language arts class, we were drafting persuasive essays about school uniforms. With thirty-two students—a mix of English Language Learners, students with ADHD, autism, and gifted learners—I decided to integrate an AI writing assistant to provide real-time feedback.

"To be clear," I said at the start, "this tool isn't here to do your writing for you. It's like having a tutor that points out ways to improve. You'll need to decide whether to use the suggestions and explain why in your reflection at the end of class."

I projected an example: a short paragraph with AI feedback. "See here," I pointed, "the AI suggests changing 'School uniforms are helpful' to 'School uniforms promote equality and reduce bullying.' It's a good suggestion because it's more specific. But if you prefer your original, you can stick with it—just explain your choice in your reflection."

Each student had a Chromebook and a feedback tracker sheet. As they revised, they documented any AI suggestions they used, why they used them, and what they rejected. I noticed Elena, an English Language Learner, working on her essay about school uniforms. She submitted a paragraph to the AI and reviewed the feedback:

"Consider rephrasing: 'Uniforms make discipline better' could become 'Uniforms improve student discipline by reducing distractions.'" Elena nodded and typed the revision, then wrote on her tracker: "I changed it because the new sentence is clearer."

At another table, Jaxon, who has ADHD, was stuck on his conclusion. The AI suggested summarizing the main points. Jaxon initially tried copying the AI's suggestion but paused when I came by.

"Jaxon," I said, "use this as a springboard. What do you want your conclusion to say? Start with their idea, then put it in your own words." He nodded, deleted the AI's text, and rewrote: "Uniforms are important because they help students focus, stop bullying, and make everyone equal."

Meanwhile, Olivia, a gifted student, used the AI's tone analysis. It suggested she make her introduction less formal. Instead of copying the AI's edit, Olivia added her own twist, then wrote on her tracker: "I didn't like how formal my intro sounded, so I changed it to feel friendlier."

To ensure accountability, I spent time reviewing tracker sheets during class and flagged any instances of copying without reflection. "Remember," I said as the class ended, "AI is a helper, not a shortcut. The best writing happens when you think critically about the suggestions and make them your own."

As we debriefed, Elena shared, "Writing why I used the suggestions helped me see what made sense and what didn't."

Jaxon added, "I liked that I couldn't just copy—it made me think about how I wanted to say it."

Olivia smiled. "It's like having a second pair of eyes, but I still get to be the writer."

By keeping all the work in class, I ensured that I could support students as they learned how to use this new tool appropriately. The tracker sheets and reflection process taught them to use AI ethically and effectively, turning the experience into a valuable learning opportunity.

Plussing

What Is It?

We can learn so much about creative thinking, voice, and choice from the world of improv. The language used here, plussing, can be attributed to Pixar's Randy Nelson. In an Edutopia YouTube video, Nelson discusses what Pixar learned about creativity and collaboration from improv. This video was shared with Erin in a graduate course she took with Dr. Robert Kelly. Nelson explores the connection between improv and collaboration: "...So you know on a team, that anything anybody says to you, you're going to get a chance to plus that. You're going to get a chance to have that be on the table. And they're going to try and make you look good, not make you look bad. At Pixar, what we mean by plussing is this: You take a piece of work. You take something that you're working on collaboratively, and when it's given to you, you don't judge it. You don't go, 'Ooh, this is pretty good. Here's what I'm going to do to make it better.' Or, 'This isn't so good, here is how I'm going to fix it.' You say, 'Here's where I'm starting. What can I do with this? How do I plus this? How do I accept the offer and make my partner look good?'" (Edutopia, 2010).

Plussing is more of an attitude and way of being than an actual strategy, but it's so powerful that it merits its own mention. Plussing is a tool that should be applied during any kind of idea generation activity. Plussing means that we encourage our students to avoid judging an idea for a little while and instead see what we can add to it or do with it. It's an optimistic stance where the basic assumption is that the idea we're starting with is a good one.

Why Do It? Peeling Back the Pedagogy

The practice of plussing adds so much to our classrooms. First and foremost, it's a culture-building tool. As we help our students get into the habit of assuming ideas come to us with potential, we are creating a classroom where people say, "Yes!" This optimism is contagious in our community. In terms of idea generation, when we make an assumption that an idea is a place we can start from rather than something we should judge, we can take ideas and grow them. This creates an expansiveness where ideas flourish.

How to Do It

When engaging in brainstorming, set brainstorming rules. One of the rules is "plussing": Add to ideas, do not detract from them. Adopt an attitude of "yes, and…"

Many different resources on other brainstorming rules can be found in a variety of places, which can enrich the protocol of plussing. One of our favorites is in the *Design Thinking for Libraries Toolkit* (p. 62), which is freely available online.

The Tool in Practice

My grade four students were sitting in a circle, about to come up with ideas for a skit on community helpers. Before we began, I reminded them, "Remember, friends, when we brainstorm ideas, we never say 'That's a bad idea!' or 'That's a good idea!' We just let an idea be an idea. Once we have lots of ideas, we can decide which ideas we want to use in our skits. Are we ready? Let's start! We're going to go around our circle and I'm going to ask each of you to share an idea about a community helper."

We went around the circle, and students shared their ideas.

"A police officer." Heads nodded.

"A doctor!" A couple of students sighed because this was the community helper they were about to suggest.

"A nurse!"

"A teacher!" I could see students thinking hard as they tried to come up with other helpers who hadn't been mentioned.

"A construction worker!" A few faces scrunched up, students clearly thinking hard about this idea. Were construction workers helpers? The students weren't sure. A few of them looked at me quizzically.

"I don't think a construction worker is a helper!" one student remarked.

"Well, what do we remember about plussing?" I asked.

"We can add to ideas but not judge them!"

"Right. So how can we plus 'construction worker'?" I asked.

"A construction worker who fixes a pothole so everyone can be safe!" suggested one of the students.

"Great plussing! We added to the idea instead of taking away from it! Let's keep going."

We continued around the circle, thinking of people who help in our communities. Our plussing protocol let us add to roles that might not typically be seen as helpers and think of ways all kinds of people contribute to our communities. And the ideas my students came up with were far better and more interesting than they would have been without this protocol.

Time Management Strategies

What Is It?

When we assign students projects with voice and choice built in, we need to also support them in developing the skills necessary to manage these kinds of projects. This can be quite a steep learning curve, especially when students haven't been given opportunities to plan their own projects before. Scaffolding students' ability to manage their time in order to achieve their goal is crucial for student success. The strategies we share here are several modest ideas you can adopt in your classroom in order to support students in managing their time in student-designed or co-designed projects.

Why Do It? Peeling Back the Pedagogy

We know that "soft skills" really are make-or-break skills in human beings; they're often what prevent people from achieving their potential. They're exceedingly important in the world of work for all of us living in the 21st Century. Time management is one of the most important ones. Being able to manage one's time keeps people focused on achieving their goals and helps them make incremental progress during each working session.

How to Do It

We will share several ideas of time management strategies and tools that can be used with students.

Chunking

Most time management tools involve chunking in some way to break a big project or task into its parts. This allows you to tackle one part of the project at a time. Chunking has long been a part of special education, where teachers support students who struggle with executive functioning by breaking a task into smaller pieces. Teaching students to do this themselves is liberating and an incredibly useful skill. In our experience, it's something that is quite challenging for young people to do without support, particularly developing the awareness of how much time each part will take them. We often like to do this alongside students during conferencing to have some one-on-one time with each student to support them in developing this skill.

To do this with students, invite them to think of their end goal and then make a list of everything that they need to do in order to reach this goal. Encourage them to get into the minutiae. For example, if the end goal is to create a podcast positively reviewing a movie a student watched, the following chunks might be identified:

- **Write a Script.**
  - Tease the plot, identify the characters. Don't give too much away because the goal is to persuade people to watch this movie!
  - Share three or four opinions about the movie. What parts or characters stood out as being particularly good or bad and why?
  - Invite a few friends who have also seen the movie to be guests on the podcast, sharing their opinions, and script a few questions to ask them.
  - Come up with a title for the podcast.
- **Record Audio.**
  - Find a quiet space to record.
  - Access technology and find software to use to record.
  - Record the script.
  - Arrange time for the podcast guests to record their parts.
- **Edit.**
  - Edit together the audio clips.
  - Find music that suits the tone of the podcast and edit it in as theme music.

The next step is identifying how much time each chunk of the project might take. This really is personal to the student, their strengths, and their areas of growth. For one student, the writing of the script might be the part that takes the longest. For another for whom writing is an area of strength, the writing part might take them a few days of class time, and then recording and editing parts might take longer. Again, in our experience, awareness of how much time something might take is a skill most students need to be supported in.

Calendars

Give students a copy of a calendar with the deadline for the project marked on it. Support students in writing the chunks of their project in the dates leading up to the project. Giving students a calendar with the deadline marked supports students in prioritizing. In the previous example of creating a podcast, if students had all the time in the world to do this project, it might take them months. But if the deadline is in three weeks, they may find they need to sacrifice parts of the project in order to make their deadline. If they only have five classes to work on their script, maybe instead of sharing four opinions, they decide to share three. This is a real-life skill. We all have deadlines, and we all have to decide how to prioritize our time and our work in order to meet them.

Use and Refuse Technology

Technology can be a huge help for time management. You can use calendar apps, scheduling apps, and even tools like digital pomodoro timers (a time management technique that emphasizes short, uninterrupted bursts of productive work time, followed by a break). You can find and teach students how to use these digital tools to support time management. Which tools you use depends on the age of your students and the technology infrastructure of your school district.

However, it can also be a huge distraction. We can all relate to sitting down to do some work and then realizing we've spent the last five minutes scrolling through Instagram. Helping students who have cell phones become aware of how they spend their time on their phones can be a good time management strategy. Invite students to reflect about how much they use their phones and what they use them for, and explore their notifications. Suggest they keep track of how many notifications they get during a given time and from which apps. Next, invite them to develop some strategies to minimize the distractions phones can bring during work time. Students might put their phone out of reach during a given work period. They could utilize focus features on their phone, such as "Do Not Disturb" mode. As mentioned, they could use a pomodoro timer app, some of which restrict access to other apps for the duration of the timer.

The Tool in Practice

In our grade-seven classroom, I pulled a stool up next to Aimee's desk. She had her project planning sheet on her desk in front of her, along with her laptop opened beside it. She had been planning a project where she would be designing a website about a topic of her choice. Aimee chose *Demon Slayer,* her favorite anime, as her topic.

On the back of her planning sheet, there was a table with empty spaces to fill in.

Chunk It Out	
Instructions: Identify the small steps that will help you accomplish your goal. Write them out in the chart below.	**Check When Complete**
Step 1:	❏
Step 2:	❏
Step 3:	❏
Step 4:	❏
Step 5:	❏
Step 6:	❏
Done!	❏

"Do you need some help chunking it out, Aimee?" I whispered.

"Yeah," she replied. "I don't get how to do this."

"Okay, so we want to figure out what are the steps that will lead you towards your goal. Think about your goal of creating a website. What's the first thing you will need to do?"

"Hmm. Come up with some ideas, I guess," she said.

"Exactly. I'll write *Brainstorming* as Step 1. What's next?" I asked, as I jotted down Brainstorming on her planning sheet.

"Uh, I need to choose a template for my website. And figure out what my pages will be called."

"Yep. Let's call that Planning," I said. I wrote *Planning* as Step 2, and scribbled a few notes about choosing a template and organizing the pages. "What's next?"

"I have to write."

"You do. Will you add pictures as you write or will that come after?"

"I think during. As I write something, I can find a related picture to include."

"Great. What's after that?"

"Editing."

"Yes. Do you want to get some peer feedback at that point? You could ask a friend to look at your site and give you some feedback."

"Okay," she said. I wrote down her ideas on her chunking sheet.

"This looks great. Are we missing any steps?" I asked her.

"I don't think so."

"Perfect! You can get started on Step 1! And don't forget to check it off when it's complete," I said. "Have fun!"

As I rolled my stool away to chat with another student, I watched Aimee pull out her sticky notes and start brainstorming some ideas for her website.

Skill Builders

What Is It?

Skill builders are activities that allow students to build the foundation that they need to successfully engage in more complex choice-based activities. These skill builders can happen individually, in small groups, or as a whole class. What makes them unique is that they are highly focused and immediately relevant. They focus on a single skill, with immediate application and practice. Whatever skill the student is learning is something they need for the task they are working on right now.

Why Do It? Peeling Back the Pedagogy

These tools are rooted in the idea that students learn best when new skills or knowledge are introduced at the exact moment they are needed for meaningful application. This approach supports Vygotsky's theory of the zone of proximal development, where learning occurs most effectively when students receive guidance on tasks that are just beyond their independent capabilities.

By identifying and addressing knowledge gaps in real time, teachers make the learning immediately relevant and practical. This approach also supports cognitive engagement, as students are more likely to retain knowledge when they see its direct connection to their goals. Additionally, these tools promote a responsive classroom environment where instruction adapts dynamically to students' needs.

Skill builders ensure students achieve understanding at lower cognitive levels before tackling higher-order thinking skills. They reinforce a growth mindset by encouraging students to view challenges as opportunities for improvement. Immediate remediation supports equitable learning by ensuring all students can access the same level of rigor, while choice in how students demonstrate their learning fosters engagement and self-efficacy.

Together, these strategies share a focus on:

- Differentiation: They meet students where they are and allow them to progress at their own pace.
- Student Agency: By integrating choice and real-time feedback, these methods empower students to take ownership of their learning.
- Meaningful Application: They connect skills and knowledge to practical, relevant tasks, which strengthens retention and engagement.
- Equity and Access: These approaches accommodate diverse learners, ensuring all students have the tools they need to succeed.

How to Do It

There are a variety of ways to build skills. Here are some of our favorites.

Online Tutorials

One of the things that we have discovered in our classrooms is that, while many of our students are avid consumers of technology and digital media, they don't always know how to use or create them. This is especially true with an online tutorial. Video tutorials are a great way to flip the classroom and support extensive choice, but first you need to make sure your students know how to use them. We like to start with a low-cognition task to teach the skill. A basic "how to draw" tutorial works but you can also incorporate a bit more choice here.

Write the key parts of successfully following an online tutorial on the board:

- Use the video pause/play button. You can also just click in the middle of the video to pause and resume playing, or use the spacebar key.
- Use the scroll bar under the video to replay portions of the video that you want to watch again.

Curate a list of simple activity-based tutorials that use materials you have available. For example:

- How to build a LEGO duck.
- How to draw an eye.
- How to fold an origami frog.
- How to do the hustle.
- How to finger knit.
- How to write a limerick.

Allow each student to choose a task and let small groups work together to support each other. When they are finished, they then find a tutorial that will help them on their next project. Once a student has used a tutorial, ask them if they would recommend it to their peers. This will also help you build your toolkit!

Just-in-Time Teaching

When a student comes to you with an idea for a project and they don't know what they don't know, you teach it. This is sometimes referred to as a "teachable moment", but we have found it to be a bit more than that.

For example:

- Imagine a student is interested in the connections between the novel *Emma* and the movie *Clueless*. You can provide a brief one-on-one lesson on character archetypes using a note catcher from your files. This gives the student a framework for their analysis.
- As students design their own language arts projects, you may notice that a number of students are analyzing song lyrics. At this point you can pause, gather all the students who want to look at lyrics, pre-teach some literary analysis vocabulary related to lyrical poetry using a flat sheet, and approve the projects before continuing on.
- In math, students are using scale measurements to prepare chalk murals for the compound. If you see students struggling with their grids, pause the whole class and review how to use a ruler.

These are all examples of how you can support choice-based work in your classroom by providing essential skills and knowledge when students need them and can use and apply them, making the learning meaningful and memorable.

The key considerations for this tool focus on readiness, flexibility, and targeted instruction. When evaluating how to progress with a skill-building activity, consider the following:

Responsiveness to Student Needs

- Identify gaps in knowledge or skills as students progress with their projects or work.
- Be attentive to both individual and group patterns of struggle or confusion.

Alignment with Curriculum and Goals

- Ensure the support aligns with learning outcomes or broader competencies students are expected to achieve. For example, teaching literary analysis vocabulary aligns with English outcomes related to textual analysis.

Preparation for the Unexpected

- Maintain a toolkit of adaptable resources (e.g., graphic organizers, note catchers, step-by-step guides) to use for mini-lessons.
- Anticipate common challenges for specific project types or subject areas.

Efficient Time Management

- Balance supporting individual students and addressing common challenges that may require a pause for the whole group.
- Strategically schedule interventions to minimize disruptions to a student's workflow.

Empowering Independence

- Offer tools and frameworks that students can apply independently once taught (e.g., a guide for analyzing lyrics or a using a ruler for scaling).
- Foster a culture where students feel comfortable seeking help without fear of judgment. Know that you will often need to reteach a skill.

How to Make It Happen

1. **Observe and Assess Needs.**
   a. Pay attention to questions, challenges, or patterns emerging during project work.
   b. Use informal check-ins, project proposals, or small group discussions to identify knowledge or skill gaps.
2. **Provide Targeted, Timely Support.**
   a. One-on-One Teaching: Offer individualized instruction for unique or niche challenges.
   b. Small Group Lessons: When several students share a similar need, gather them and provide a focused mini-lesson.
   c. Whole-Class Interventions: If an issue impacts the majority, pause the class and address it directly.
3. **Prepare and Use Flexible Resources.**
   a. Maintain a library of "ready-to-go" resources for common concepts or skills.
   b. Create tools that are adaptable across subjects and projects, such as universal graphic organizers or checklists.
4. **Reinforce through Application.**
   a. Ensure students immediately apply what they've learned to their work, solidifying the concept in a meaningful context.
5. **Monitor and Adjust.**
   a. After each intervention, check back to see how effectively students are using the new knowledge or skill.
   b. Collect feedback to refine your just-in-time teaching process. Do the students need additional scaffolding? Did the group lesson resonate?

6. **Foster Independence.**
    a. Teach students how to identify when they "don't know what they don't know." Encourage them to ask for clarification or help when they get stuck.
    b. Provide a structure for reflective planning to help students outline what they need before diving into projects.

Mastery to Move

This teaching tool requires students to demonstrate mastery of a skill or a concept before they can begin to use it in a project. For example, you might have students complete a quiz on literary devices before they can begin their choice novel. If students do not demonstrate mastery, they are immediately offered support through reteaching and practice. One resource we recommend for teachers wanting to learn more about Mastery Based Learning is the Modern Classroom Project.

Key considerations for this tool centre on clear benchmarks for mastery, effective assessment, and immediate support for students who are not successful.

Define Mastery Clearly.

- Establish clear criteria for mastery of the skill or concept. For example, mastery might mean scoring 80% or higher on a quiz or demonstrating a specific level of proficiency on a rubric.
- Ensure the criteria are aligned with curricular outcomes and communicated to students.

Balance Accountability and Support.

- Emphasize that mastery is a stepping stone, not a gatekeeping mechanism. Students who do not meet the standard should receive immediate, constructive support to help them succeed.

Scaffold Learning.

- Provide opportunities to build toward mastery through incremental steps such as practice tasks or formative assessments.
- Offer varied ways to demonstrate understanding, such as quizzes, verbal explanations, or practical demonstrations.

Foster a Growth Mindset.

- Normalize the idea that mastery takes time and that remediation is an opportunity to learn, not a setback.
- Build a culture of perseverance and self-improvement.

How to Make It Happen

- **Set Clear Mastery Goals.**
    - Define the specific skill or concept students need to master before moving on.
    - Create an assessment that accurately measures the skill, such as a quiz, performance task, or checklist.

- **Provide Formative Practice.**
    - Offer practice tasks that align with the mastery goals, allowing students to build confidence and familiarity before the formal assessment.

- **Assess for Mastery.**
    - Administer a quiz, task, or checkpoint to evaluate student readiness. Ensure the assessment provides actionable feedback.

- **Offer Immediate Remediation.**
  - For students who don't demonstrate mastery, provide timely and targeted support.
  - Allow students to reassess once they've completed remediation.

- **Enable Mastery to Lead to Application.**
  - When students demonstrate mastery, guide them in applying the skill to a meaningful project.

Sample Applications

ELA: Students must identify and explain the effects of three literary devices in a poem before analyzing devices in their choice novel.

Math: Students demonstrate mastery of graphing linear equations on a coordinate plane before applying the skill to a real-world problem such as designing a map.

Science: Students complete a lab safety quiz with 100% accuracy before participating in hands-on experiments.

Social Studies: Students match key terms and events to their historical significance before starting a group debate on historical perspectives.

The Tool in Practice

Online Tutorials

I curated a list of simple tutorials that didn't need much prep: how to draw a cube, fold an origami frog, or build a LEGO duck. "Pick one," I told students, "and focus on following the steps. You can work in pairs if you want."

Luis, whose first language was Spanish, chose the origami frog tutorial. I noticed him watching intently but struggling to keep up with the video's pace. "Luis," I said quietly, crouching next to him. "You can pause and replay parts whenever you need to. Have you tried turning on the subtitles?"

He shook his head. I showed him how to enable English subtitles on the video, and his expression brightened as the steps became clearer to him. "You can also look for tutorials in Spanish," I added. "That might help with understanding the instructions."

He nodded and tried again, this time pausing between each fold and using the subtitles to follow along. By the end, he held up his finished frog—not perfect, but definitely recognizable—and gave me a small smile. "I think I understand now."

"Great work," I said. "Now, for our next step, let's find a tutorial that can help you with the bedroom project," a math project they were working on using 2D shapes and area. "You'll need to know how to create accurate grids, draw 2D shapes, and work with measurements."

Luis searched for a video about drawing grids. The next day, he showed me his work—a carefully measured and labeled grid for his bedroom design. "This one's good," he said, showing me the tutorial link. "I think others could use it too."

"That's excellent," I said. "Add it to the class list, and if you're ready, start brainstorming how you'll lay out your room."

By the end of the week, students were working on their projects, choosing how to demonstrate their understanding of perimeter and area; some drew scaled grids, others created 3D sketches, and there were even some LEGO models.

Just-in-Time Teaching

As I sat down with Aria to discuss her choice novel, *The Giver*, I asked her to choose a character she found most interesting and tell me about the author's techniques of characterization. Without hesitation, she said, "Jonas. He's brave, but also unsure about what's right sometimes." I could tell she understood the novel well but was unsure about the academic vocabulary I was using.

"Interesting observation," I commented, leaning forward. "Can you show me where in the text you see that?"

Aria flipped through her book with practiced precision. "Here," she said, pointing to a passage where Jonas hesitates to share his feelings during a family conversation. "This shows he's unsure. He doesn't say everything he's thinking."

"Exactly," I said. "That's indirect characterization—it's not directly stated, but we see it in his actions. Now, can you find an example of direct characterization?"

She seemed more confident now and flipped further back. "This part," she said, reading aloud: "'Jonas was careful about language.' That's pretty direct, right?"

"Absolutely! That's direct characterization because the narrator tells us outright about Jonas's personality," I said. "Both kinds work together to give us a fuller picture of who he is."

Aria smiled, clearly proud of herself. "So, indirect is like figuring it out yourself, and direct is like being told?"

Mastery to Move

As my grade nines settled into their seats, I handed out the "Mastery Check" on chemical reactions. Each student needed to identify and classify five types of reactions—synthesis, decomposition, single replacement, double replacement, and combustion—before starting their choice project. The project options ranged from creating an instructional video on reaction types to designing a comic strip illustrating the reactions in a real-world scenario.

Most students breezed through the check-in, but when I looked at Sara's quiz, I noticed she had mixed up single and double replacement reactions. "Hey, Sara," I said, pulling a chair up beside her. "Let's review this together. What's happening in this equation?"

She squinted at the example and hesitated. "I think it's double replacement because two things are switching places?"

"You're close," I said. "But take another look—only one element is being swapped out. That's a single replacement."

We worked through a few more examples, and I gave her a new set of practice questions. After ten minutes, she grinned. "I've got it now!" She retook the mastery check, passing with flying colors.

"Great job, Sara," I said. "Now, which project are you thinking of tackling?"

She lit up. "I want to make the comic strip! I already have an idea for how to show a combustion reaction in action."

"Awesome," I said. "I can't wait to see what you come up with."

PART 3

Teaching Protocols and Task Design

We want to begin this part with a key philosophical assumption that underlies a teaching approach that prioritizes student voice and choice. Since you made the choice to pick up this book, we suspect that this assumption is one you make, too. It's important to draw attention to this assumption explicitly, however, in order to understand the pedagogy behind the ideas we share in this chapter.

We believe that teachers are designers of learning. It is essential that you, too, believe this if you wish to prioritize student voice and choice. Borrowing from concepts of design thinking, we understand teaching as a complex, creative, and iterative process (Scott and Lock, 2022). Good teaching begins with many questions: Who are my students? What do they need to learn? What are they coming here with? What am I supposed to teach them? What's most essential? How can I reach them? What do I do to make sure they know it? How do they show it? How do I know that they know it? What do I do then? Teachers who think of themselves as designers of learning consider all these questions and make judgments and best guesses given what they know to figure out a journey that will help their students learn. We also assume that teacher-designers are reflexive and use experience and feedback to iterate their teaching to flex to the needs of their students as they arise and to redesign when something doesn't go the way they intended.

The strategies we share in this chapter will support you in designing learning tasks that incorporate voice and choice. When you are sitting down to design a learning task or a unit, the easiest way to start is by beginning from the lens of voice and choice. Begin with the first two questions: Who are my students? What do they need to learn? Then your task becomes how you can connect these two dots. Thinking about your students and how you can make a topic interesting and engaging to them requires you to know them and your topic well. Choice is inherent in how you will reach them, however, because we know we can make generalizations about a group of students, but the individuality of each student in your class is why choice is so powerful. What's engaging to one is not engaging to another. Providing students with choices within your task design is what will allow you to reach more of your students.

You may be thinking about task design for a current task or unit you have used previously, and be considering ways that you could incorporate more voice and choice within it. You can take any of the strategies in this chapter and fold them into a current unit or task to incorporate more voice and choice. You can — and should — fold these tools into your existing work. This is how you will begin to incorporate more voice and choice tomorrow.

We hope that this part, and this book, will give you the tools you need to start designing your teaching with the lens of voice and choice from the ground up because this will be more effective and will produce greater results. In this process, you should also be modeling active learning by inviting your students into the work. Ask them what you should do differently next time. Our students have grown to love that question, especially when we good-naturedly acknowledge that they will see no benefit from their feedback, but that next year's students will really appreciate it. It is one more way to give them agency and for them to see that their voice can have an impact.

Building tasks and units from the ground up is a time-consuming but valuable process that you can engage in once you feel some comfort in the kinds of strategies and protocols we share in this chapter.

We teacher-designers know that we have constraints that impact how and what we design. We need to consider how much time we have, the structure of the student timetable, the curriculum we must teach, the needs of our students and community, and the attitudes of our stakeholders, among them parents and administration. Though it seems counterintuitive, we actually believe these constraints enable you to incorporate *more* student voice. Designing around these constraints means the tasks you create will be more personalized to your students, not less. For example:

Time and Schedules

The amount of time you have available to you dictates what kinds of tasks you design for your students. It's possible to design a very short task that involves student choice if that's all the time you have.

Timetables are a structural tool that can really dictate how time is allocated. Block scheduling means big chunks of time but with short attention spans teachers need to be thoughtful about how they break up that time. This, too, means you may see your students less often. Shorter periods mean less time to dig into something but might mean you see your students more frequently. Both timetabling approaches offer considerations for how you can design engaging tasks for your students.

Curriculum

We are all beholden to certain curricular standards, be they provincially or state-mandated, or school- or district-determined. We rarely, if ever, have free rein over what we teach. The topics we are obligated to teach our students give us a place to start. Looking for how this topic can connect with our students is the place for creativity to begin. "That sounds great but I have to teach (insert mandated outcome here)" is not the end of the conversation. Every teacher then decides how they are going to teach and the two key questions that you start with are "How can I build choice into this lesson?" and "How will my students see themselves in this content?" It is not your job to re-design the curriculum but it is your job to design how the curriculum is taught and assessed. And this should be a process of continual re-design. If you are in the difficult position of having little or no say in the how of your teaching ("My department requires these tasks and these assessments" or, "I have to use the same grading formula as everyone else"), it is time to get subversive. These tools can also be used in small ways to incorporate voice and choice in highly prescriptive settings and even small steps will move you forward.

Classroom Complexity

Many students may not have the foundational skills to engage with the assigned work, leading to frustration and disengagement. This often manifests as challenging behaviours. It is essential to move beyond compliance as the prerequisite to participation. Creating tasks that allow for different methods of engagement meets students where they are and moves learning forward. It is essential to explicitly teach students about making choices and what it means to express preferences. And then you have to listen. Highly confident learners are usually capable of asking for the differentiation they need. In complex learners that same request often looks like non-compliance. While it is challenging to implement voice and choice in settings where students are struggling to meet behavior expectations, it is not only possible but necessary. Voice and choice should not be seen as a reward for compliance but as a fundamental part of the learning process. By prioritizing agency over compliance, we cultivate a more inclusive learning community.

Competing Demands

Schools are wildly busy places, full of competing demands. It's easy to give into the panic that can be a low hum in schools: How can I offer my students choice if they can't read? How on earth can I ask my students to be involved in the decision making in our classroom if I have a student who is so dysregulated he's throwing books and banging on lockers? We don't pretend these competing demands don't exist. But it is possible to design with them in mind.

Stakeholders

Teaching and learning don't happen in a vacuum. In fact, we have many stakeholders in the work we do. Considering the interests and strengths of our community members, parent population, larger community, administration, and politicians can determine where and how we can infuse student voice and choice in our learning. Sometimes this might mean we have to start small, and this is absolutely okay.

When we consider these constraints as a place to begin when incorporating voice and choice into our task design, possibilities emerge. As busy professionals, it's tempting to look for "one-size-fits-all" projects or tasks we can plop into our planning and deliver to students. That's not what we're offering here because we know this doesn't work. Instead, we encourage you to look at the constraints in your own unique situation to design an approach that works for you and your students.

Our Process of Task Design

Through our years of working together, we have developed processes we use to design tasks that incorporate voice and choice. We usually start with our curriculum, which we try to read in a generous way. What exactly is this curriculum asking us to teach? What assumptions do we make about this? For example, our curriculum might never actually ask students to write an essay. It might ask them to engage in literary analysis. When we really get clear about what our curriculum is asking of us and our students, possibilities emerge. There are many different paths we can take toward literary analysis when we aren't committed to having students write a formal essay. Sometimes, expectations get downloaded from a higher grade to a lower grade. For example, if in grade ten students must write an essay, grade nine teachers think they must teach their students to write an essay, even though this is not asked of them in their curriculum. Instead, we should be teaching our students the skills and processes that will later support them in writing a formal essay.

We have engaged in purposeful processes and activities in which we got to know our students, their interests, and their preferences, many of which we have outlined in Part 1. We come to our brainstorming sessions equipped with this knowledge of our students.

In the next step of our process, we use the same aids that we invite our students to use. We employ tools such as brainstorming, affinity mapping, and heat mapping to come up with possibilities, look for commonalities and trends, and narrow down our ideas to something viable. We often start by throwing a bunch of ideas onto sticky notes. At this point, we resist the temptation to just go with our first good idea. We are purposeful in making sure we give ourselves lots of time for this part of task design as we know we need processing time before making a decision. We find it often helps to take our rough ideas for a walk. A quick loop around the outside of the school can help us to gain a new perspective or get unstuck. And if not, we feel better for the fresh air and are ready to get back at it.

Remember, creativity is a skill. You have to practice it to get better at it. If you haven't had a lot of opportunity to be creative with your curriculum this might be challenging and uncomfortable. We are better in the company of our peers so work with your teaching partners. If you don't have partners at school, go online. There are so many virtual communities that you can join but you can also search the internet to get inspired and see what other creators are doing. Don't limit yourself to just teachers' communities. Analogous research can help you see solutions and innovations that you hadn't even imagined (Cass and Sanderson, 2019). We often characterize ourselves as magpies, collecting bright and shiny things wherever we see them because you never know what will spark your next great idea. We are purposeful in involving ourselves in different activities and topics, especially if our students are into them, to get inspired in this way. For example, when we began designing social studies tasks using games, we began playing Dungeons & Dragons. We came up with so many great ideas for our tasks once D&D opened us to a range of game mechanics we'd never experienced before. When designing a task connected to an analogous field, we also make sure we talk to the experts. In this same example, Tara met with an acquaintance who was really into board games to learn more about other interesting games we could play to get more ideas to incorporate into our design. Depending on what you teach, these analogous fields may involve people who work within the disciplines out in the world. Where does math live in our world? Where are the scientists? What are they doing? Finding and connecting with these people can be rich grounds for inspiration.

This is a great place to add in one of our favorite caveats: "Cool idea, bro. So what?" We've been known to run away with a really great idea only to realize later that we'd gone way into left field. Once you think you have something that you want to move forward with, come back to your curriculum and learner outcomes. Are you meeting your curricular goals? Is the work directly connected to the learner outcomes? Do students have the skills they need to be successful? If not, how will you teach them? How are you going to assess this work with the students? Where is the choice in the work? Is it meaningful and authentic choice? How are your students' voices reflected and elevated through the work? This is the point in the process when you need to ground yourself in the essential learning. Identifying it and using it to ground your work can also help to solve disagreements and resolve uncertainties. It is the non-negotiable to return to throughout the design process. This is all the more reason you need to make sure you give yourself ample time to design your task because your first idea will not (and should not!) likely be your last one.

When we disagree about which option to choose, we ask ourselves which option best serves and achieves the desired outcome. This often requires us to leave our egos at the door. We both have very strong personalities and opinions, but when we disagree, we have to return to one thing: our belief in our students and centring them in the task design. As teachers, we must also be comfortable with taking risks and allowing for the possibility that there is another way to be successful. Don't make decisions out of fear. Too often as teachers, when we are challenged with a new way of doing something we react with a laundry list of possible negative outcomes. "That will never work for my students because…" Allow for the possibility of success. What if it's amazing? And then plan to make it happen. We have all worked with a colleague who has a problem for every solution. This work requires you to have solutions for every problem.

Once we have narrowed our ideas down to one to pursue, we often engage in a workflow where we come together, delegate, and then come back together. We work through the steps we need to in order to create the teaching and learning materials our students need, always making sure we come back to each other to check our work, incorporate each other's perspective, and iterate our designs before we share them with our students.

The step of the actual teaching happens next, which differs widely depending on what it is we've created. A final step we always incorporate into our task design is reflection and iteration. We always keep a running document in our Google Folder called "Changes for Next Time," the idea of which we've also borrowed from the field of design thinking. We consider our task design a prototype that can and should always evolve. In our document, we keep track of unintended consequences of our design choices or new ways we could progress forward that only emerge when we prototype our idea. This document often also includes suggestions from our students. When we come back to the task design the next year, we always look at this document first.

Voice and choice are not a panacea that will fix all the problems in your classroom. However, our goal as educators should always be empowerment. Voice and choice are one way we can empower kids. When we do this as a regular part of our task design, our students understand that they have agency and power. They know they can control aspects of their own lives and choices. In a world where too often it feels like choices are being removed from us, this is more important than ever.

Affinity Mapping

What Is It?

Affinity mapping is a strategy the education world has borrowed from the design world. The affinity diagram was devised by Jiro Kawakita, a Japanese anthropologist, in the 1960s. It is also referred to as the KJ Method. Affinity mapping is a way to organize ideas into categories. Unlike typical brainstorming where the categories might dictate the ideas, affinity mapping works in the opposite way. Ideas are generated and then from these ideas, the categories emerge.

Why Do It? Peeling Back the Pedagogy

Affinity mapping is useful in creative exercises where you want your students to generate many ideas. Research in the field of creative development affirms that the more ideas that are generated, the more potential there is for an interesting, original idea to appear (Kelly, 2016). When students generate many ideas for the purpose of later choosing one to pursue, they are learning that ideas are not precious (Kelly, 2016). Often when students are given an opportunity to choose a topic or a method for a project, they will choose something familiar — a topic they already know a lot about, or a type of presentation they've done before. The end result may be enjoyable for students, but the project doesn't often push their boundaries or allow them to attempt something new. Affinity mapping is one way we can encourage our students to look beyond the obvious and find an idea that's fresh and exciting.

Once ideas are generated, they are generally no good to students unless they are organized. As the affinity mapping protocol is used, the categories to organize the data emerge. These categories allow students to make sense of the ideas generated. Because ideas are tangible and movable — we like sticky notes and a big, empty wall for this protocol — when the ideas are moved around and connections are made, students can see the categories in which they have more ideas, and the categories in which they have fewer ideas, which can help them see ideas with more potential.

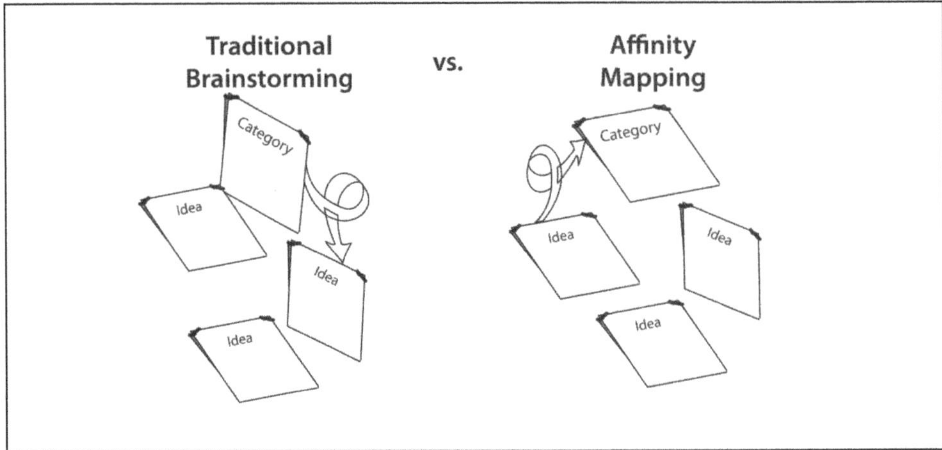

How to Do It

Materials Needed
- Sticky notes
- Sharpies/pens
- Chart paper or empty wall space

Protocol
1. Give students a topic that you wish them to generate many ideas about.
2. Set a time limit. The age of your students may impact how long you wish them to brainstorm for. You generally want your time limit to be tight enough that students won't get bored and start getting off task, but long enough that interesting, less obvious ideas will emerge. For older students, a time limit of five to fifteen minutes is ideal. For younger students, two to five minutes might be more appropriate. Set a timer for the appropriate number of minutes.
3. Distribute a stack of sticky notes and a marker to each student. Explain the task and be sure to tell students that the objective is to come up with the most ideas possible in the time given. Remind students that they should not be self-censoring their ideas at this time. Tell them that they should be recording one idea per sticky note.

4. When the time is up, gather students together around chart paper or wall space. This can be done as a whole class or in small groups. Invite a student to share one of their ideas and place it on the chart paper or wall space.
5. Invite the next student to share one of their ideas. Ask the student: Is this idea similar to the one already shared or different? If it is similar, the student will cluster their idea next to the idea it is similar to. If it is different, they will place their sticky note on its own in another area of the wall space.
6. Continue inviting students to share ideas and cluster them with other ideas that they have something in common with.
7. Discuss what you might name each category. At this point, sticky notes might be further moved around or subcategorized. Write the category names on the chart paper or on a different-colored sticky note.
8. You might invite discussion around what students notice about the affinity map. Which clusters have more sticky notes? Why? Which clusters have fewer sticky notes? Why? Where are there connections between clusters?

From here, you can have individual students select an idea to pursue further. They can select an idea they contributed or one their classmates contributed. This further emphasizes that ideas are meant to be shared.

The Tool in Practice

I wanted my grade-eight students to create water conservation campaigns as part of our science unit on water systems. They needed to choose a water conservation issue they cared about, and I decided to use affinity mapping to generate ideas for awareness campaigns. Armed with sticky notes and markers, I set a timer for ten minutes and gave my students a few instructions.

"Remember," I explained, "we've already come up with lots of examples of how human actions impact water quality and quantity. They're up there on the board. Let's read this list again. We've got the overuse of fresh water in cities and on farms, leaky taps and toilets, pollution from agriculture and industry, deforestation, climate change leading to more evaporation of water, and littering in oceans and lakes.

"Now it's your turn to see if we can figure out a way to prevent this or slow it down. For the next ten minutes, your job is to come up with as many solutions to these problems as possible. Your solutions could be about raising awareness or could be technological or physical ways we could prevent these problems from happening, slow them down, or reverse them.

"Don't censor yourself. Write it down even if you think it's a dumb idea or one that other people have come up with before. One idea per sticky note! Are you ready? Go!"

I wandered around the room as heads went down and all I could hear was the scratch of marker on paper. Occasionally, students looked up to think, then bent back down as a new idea came to mind. The timer went off.

"Awww!" one student exclaimed. "I just got another idea!"

"Write it down, quick!" I said. The student scribbled something on a pink sticky note.

I explained the next step. "Okay, so now I want you to get into groups of three or four. I want you to take turns sharing your ideas with your group. As you share, I want you to sort your ideas. If an idea is similar to another idea, place them together. If it's different, place it apart. It's up to you to determine the criteria for what makes an idea similar or different. It's okay if you have single sticky notes hanging out there all by themselves. What clarifying questions do you have before we begin? Okay, go!"

I walked from group to group, listening as students shared and sorted their ideas, supporting where needed. After all the sticky notes had been sorted within small groups, we gathered around a big empty whiteboard. I asked a group to share one of their clusters.

"We have a bunch of sticky notes here about social media, like using Instagram or TikTok to show people how to save water at home," one student offered.

"Do any other groups have similar clusters?" I asked.

"Yeah, we do!"

"Us too. Does YouTube count as social media?" We had a quick discussion about that question and decided that most YouTube videos that were more informative than persuasive should be put in their own category.

I continued asking groups to share their clusters, organizing as we went. By the end of class, the whiteboard was covered in colorful sticky notes, grouped under category titles: social media campaigns, posters, robotic devices, ideas to reduce plastic use, devices to capture chemical runoff from agriculture, devices to reduce water use at home, children's books about conserving water, videos to profile an issue or concern, and more. I invited students to do a silent gallery walk, observing what their classmates had come up with.

The next day, we gathered around the whiteboard once more. "Now that you've had a chance to sleep on it, I want you to choose one of these ideas. Over the next couple of weeks, you will work with a partner to make this idea a reality and create a working prototype of the idea to test. I really want you to choose something you care about. We have tons of great ideas here. You can pick one that you came up with or one of your classmates' ideas. And it's more than okay if two groups do the same idea! You will probably come up with different ways to approach it, and that's a good thing!"

Eyes lit up as students realized they were going to build and test one of the great ideas they had brainstormed. I stepped back and watched as pairs of students scanned the wall, removed sticky notes, considered their options, and made decisions. One thing I knew for sure: they weren't lacking possibilities. Every single student in the class now had an idea.

Sample affinity map

Brainstorming Possibilities

What Is It?

We can give students more credit than we often do. If we hand over the task of brainstorming and planning projects that meet learner outcomes over to our students, engagement soars. Often the projects that students come up with aren't all that different from ideas we might come up with for them. Sometimes, though, they'll surprise us and come up with something completely original.

Why Do It? Peeling Back the Pedagogy

One of the biggest benefits of incorporating more voice and choice into our teaching practice is the agency it gives students over their learning. The more agency they have, the more engaged they will be. And that's when you might notice the state of flow that psychologist Mihaly Csikszentmihalyi (1996) wrote about, when time seems to disappear because engagement in the task is so high. To be honest, flow is quite difficult to achieve in school because we have to do so many things not because we want to but because we are required to. We have found that the moments when flow does show up are almost exclusively in times when students have designed their own learning tasks or approaches to accomplishing a goal.

Before they can have agency, however, students must be supported in making choices that align with their own interests, skills, and prior knowledge. That's why a formalized brainstorming session can be very helpful here.

How to Do It

There are many different ways to accomplish the goal of having students brainstorm ways to meet a learning goal. We will outline a few below. It is a good idea to establish some brainstorming rules before beginning. As mentioned earlier, we like the rules outlined in *Design Thinking for Libraries* (p. 62).

Collaborative Brainstorm

1. Begin with a desired learning outcome. Write the learning outcome on the whiteboard or project it for the class to see.
2. Place students in small groups. Give each group a large piece of paper or some whiteboard space.
3. Instruct the students to write the learning outcome in the centre of their space.
4. Invite the students to create a mind map, brainstorming as many tasks as they can think of to meet the learning outcome as they can and record all their ideas on their map.
5. Post the different brainstorm maps around the room and invite students to do a gallery walk to view the different ideas others who were not in their group came up with.

Speed Dating

This idea was shared with Erin in a graduate course by Dr. Robert Kelly. He published the strategy in his book *Creative Development* (2016).

1. Clear a space in the room by moving tables and desks. Set up chairs in two concentric circles, with the ring of inner chairs facing the outer chairs. You want as many chairs as there are students. Get students to sit in the chairs.

2. Give students the learning outcome. Invite them to begin by independently brainstorming a few ideas about activities they could do to achieve the outcome. Have them record their ideas in a notebook. Dr. Kelly reminds us that you never want to send students to a brainstorm session "cold" — they should always warm up by having a few ideas to bring with them. This gives them somewhere to start and something to build off.

3. After students have had a chance to write a few ideas down, invite them to share with the person sitting across from them. Explain to students that if their partner suggests a good idea, they should record it on their own list. This protocol works best alongside the plussing strategy; remind students that the goal is to grow the list of ideas together with their partner. Austin Kleon (2012) reminds us to steal like an artist — combine ideas, be inspired by others, and credit where your good ideas come from. Be sure to set a timer to limit the conversation. We recommend one to two minutes per partner.

4. When the time is up, have all students move one seat to their right. The result of this is that every second person will talk to each other. Having all students move keeps the momentum going and the atmosphere lively.

Round-the-Room Brainstorming

Preparation

1. Choose Topics: Identify the main topics or subjects for brainstorming. For example, "Plant and Animal Adaptations" or "Genres of Novels."

2. Create Chart Papers: Write each topic in large, clear letters on separate pieces of chart paper. Place these around the room, leaving enough space for groups to gather comfortably.

3. Provide Materials: Ensure each chart paper has markers of different colors nearby. Assign colors to groups to track contributions, if desired.

4. Set Clear Expectations: Explain the activity to students, including rules:
   - Add new ideas to the chart paper.
   - No repeating ideas already on the paper.
   - Copy ideas from other chart papers only if they are relevant and not already listed.

5. Define Timing: Set a timer for each round (two to five minutes works well). Share that timing with students to maintain focus and urgency.

Activity Execution

1. Form Groups: Divide students into small groups (three to five students). Assign each group to a starting chart paper.

2. Brainstorm Round 1: Students brainstorm and write their ideas on their assigned chart paper. Encourage everyone to contribute.

3. Rotate Groups: After the timer goes off, instruct groups to rotate to the next chart paper. Students should read the existing ideas before adding their own.
   - Tip: You can rotate clockwise or assign a random order to keep movement dynamic.

4. Add New Ideas: Students add fresh ideas to the chart paper. They may copy relevant ideas from previous papers but cannot repeat ideas already present.

5. Repeat Rounds: Continue the process, rotating to new papers for as long as new ideas are being generated.

- Guiding Questions: After a couple of rounds, offer a question or prompt related to the topic to encourage deeper thinking. For example:
  - "What specific examples support this idea?"
  - "How could this concept relate to real life or other subjects?"

Wrap-Up

1. Return to Original Chart: Groups return to their starting chart paper to review the expanded list of ideas.
2. Reflection and Discussion: Have groups
- highlight key ideas or trends they notice;
- identify ideas they found most surprising or insightful;
- present their chart paper to the class or share highlights in a whole-group discussion.

The Tool in Practice

To Brainstorm Ideas

My grade-five students sat in two circles, facing each other. Sheena made a face at Dustin, sitting across from her. He poked his tongue out at her but shifted his focus to me as I asked for the students' attention.

"Okay, so we're going to brainstorm ideas for projects we could do to demonstrate the learner outcome, 'Investigate how oral language can be designed to communicate ideas and information.' Let's start by doing a bit of silent brainstorming. I want you to make a list in your notebook of as many ways you can think of to communicate ideas and information through oral language. I want to remind you that I expect silence and I expect that your pencil is to paper for the entire two minutes of this beginning brainstorm session. There will be opportunities to share your ideas with your partners later. Ready? Timer starts now!"

I activated the timer on my phone. Heads dropped as students crouched over the notebooks in their laps, jotting down ideas. I walked around the circles, peeking over shoulders to see what they were writing. I saw many common ideas—speeches, presentations, and stories. As the two-minute mark neared, eyes began to glance up and students started to run out of the more obvious ideas.

"All right, now I'd like you to share your ideas with the person sitting across from you. If your partner shares an idea you think is a good one, write it down and add it to your list! Don't forget that our goal is to plus good ideas—add to them and make them even better than they started out being. So feel free to brainstorm more good ideas together with your partner. You'll have two minutes to talk. I'll let you know when you have one minute left so you can make sure both people have a chance to share. Make sense? Okay, let's go!"

I started the timer again. The room buzzed with conversation as students leaned toward their partners to share. I noticed a few students pulling their chairs in closer to hear better. As I walked around the circle, I listened in on their back-and-forth: familiar ideas came up again—speeches, presentations, stories.

At the one-minute warning, something interesting happened. Most partners had finished sharing their initial ideas, so they began thinking further.

"What about YouTube videos? People talk on those. They, like, record their voiceovers and then layer it on top of the video. We could make videos for YouTube," Jamie shared. Jamie's partner, Gina, wrote it down.

"Oh yeah, and podcasts. Sometimes my family listens to podcasts when we go on road trips." Both Jamie and Gina wrote that one down, too.

"Even the ads we see on YouTube have people talking in them. We could make ads?"

I began the countdown. "Three… two… one! Time's up! Okay, say thanks to your partner, grab your notebook, and move one seat to your right. Everyone move now!"

The students stood up, shifted over, and said hello to their new partners.

"Now we just repeat this again. Share your ideas and grow them together! Ready? Go!" I started the timer once more.

By the end of our forty-five-minute period, the students had rotated through a dozen partners, and their notebooks were full of ideas—far more than they'd started with.

"Tomorrow, we'll sift through all these ideas and choose which ways you might want to tackle this learner outcome. You have a notebook *full* of great ideas to choose from!"

To Review Information

It was a Monday morning in my grade-six science class, and I could feel the expectant energy as everyone filed in. On Friday, we had written a test on the particle theory of matter, and it showed that there were some key areas we needed to solidify before moving on. That day, we were going to actively review the particle theory and how temperature changes affect the behavior of particles in solids, liquids, and gases.

"Alright, everyone," I started. "Today we're preparing for our unit test. We're going to review how temperature affects particles by working together and building on each other's ideas. You'll move around the room, adding your thoughts to chart papers about solids, liquids, and gases. By the end we'll have a massive brainstorm to help us understand these ideas better."

I had already prepped the room with six chart papers, each taped to a different wall. Two read "Solids," two read "Liquids," and two were titled "Gases." Beneath each title, I had written a guiding question:

For solids: What happens to particles in a solid when temperature increases or decreases?

For liquids: How does heating or cooling change how particles in a liquid behave?

For gases: What are the effects of temperature on gas particles?

I handed each group a marker and sent them to a starting station. "You'll have six minutes at each chart. Work together to brainstorm as many ideas as you can. Write them down—no repeats allowed! If you see an idea at another station that fits here but isn't written yet, you can add it. And remember, when we rotate, your goal is to build on what's already there."

Students rotated through the solids, liquids, and gases stations and then repeated the cycle. This meant they saw each topic twice, giving them a chance to deepen their understanding and expand their ideas.

The timer started, and the room filled with the buzz of conversation and the sound of markers on paper. At the solids station, I heard students discussing how heating makes particles vibrate faster. "That's why ice melts!" one student exclaimed, jotting it down.

Over at the liquids station, another group was on a roll: "When you cool a liquid, the particles slow down and get closer together—like water turning into ice!"

By the time the first round ended, they were ready to move. I clapped to signal the rotation. "Quickly, folks, head to the next chart!"

At the second station, students leaned in, reading the previous group's ideas before diving in with their own. "Oh, they wrote about gas particles spreading out when heated," one student at the gases station said. "We can add that the particles move so fast they escape a container—like a balloon popping!"

Students stayed actively engaged in the review while I circulated around the room with a class list on a clipboard, listening to conversations, asking questions, and observing the process. It gave me great assessment data, as students were able to demonstrate their understanding informally.

After six progressively shorter rotations, the charts were filled with colorful ideas. I brought the class back together. "Now, head back to your original chart and see what's been added. Look for patterns or ideas you hadn't thought of before."

When they returned to their starting stations, the energy was palpable. "Whoa, I didn't think about particles in a solid vibrating but staying in place!" one group said. Another marveled at how many examples their peers had added.

To wrap up, I asked each group to share two key takeaways. "Solids expand when heated because the particles vibrate more," one group said. Another added, "In gases, the particles move faster and farther apart, which makes the gas take up more space."

I stepped back and gestured to the charts now filled with ideas. "You all just created a wealth of knowledge together," I said, smiling. And the test results showed that this had been an effective review session for all learners!

Centres with Choice

What Is It?

Centres are a staple in most elementary classrooms. When set up well, they enable student-centred, engaging activities which are also self-checking and self-selecting. The activities are used to focus on a set of skills and deepen the students' knowledge and abilities in that area. Students can work alone, in pairs, or in small groups.

Why Do It? Peeling Back the Pedagogy

Centres enable students to practice skills that have been taught in class and offer the opportunity for easy differentiation. While they provide opportunities for students to show what they know in a variety of ways they also allow you to observe small groups in focused contexts, which can inform your planning and instruction. Struggling students are often more receptive to receiving extra support in smaller group situations, and with everyone engaged in their own learning, you are in a position to offer that extra help. Ensure that your students are responsible for the supplies and reset of each centre to also reinforce community and responsibility.

Centres can also be an effective strategy when there are skills or tasks to be completed. They offer the illusion of choice that is present when your mom says that you can eat your carrots first or last. You choose when, but either way, you are eating the carrots. With centres, students choose the order of the activities, but not what activities to complete.

How to Do It

While you're designing and creating your classroom stations, it's important to keep in mind that centre activities should not include new material. Instead, they should reinforce a topic you've covered together as a class. While learning centres are intended to encourage independent study, they should do so with material that students are already familiar with to solidify their understanding.

Establishing Centre Rules

- Establish clear routines and expectations for your centres. You might want to include a materials list and a visual of what it should look like when you're done.
- Be clear about how many students can be at one centre simultaneously, based on the nature of the task. For example, a microscope centre might have a maximum of two students, while a centre with math manipulatives might have room for four to six students.
- Your classroom size and the number of students will affect how many centres you might have. In a middle or high school setting four to eight usually works well.
- How will centre time end? Will everyone rotate after twenty minutes or do you move on when you have completed the task?

What Makes a Good Centre?

A great centre is more than just an activity — it's a purposeful, student-centred experience. When designing centres, think about these criteria:

- Purposeful Practice: The centre should have a clear purpose tied to specific skills or concepts. Activities that feel meaningful are more engaging for students. For example, a science centre could involve testing materials for their conductivity, tying it to a unit on electricity.
- Multi-Sensory Learning: Centres are most effective when they allow students to use a variety of senses. Hands-on materials, visuals, and even sound can deepen understanding. For example, a music centre might involve matching rhythms to instruments or composing a short melody.
- Collaboration: While centres can work for individuals, activities designed for pairs or small groups can foster teamwork and discussion. A social studies centre might involve students working together to place key historical events on a shared timeline.
- Built-In Progression: Good centres allow for differentiation, offering opportunities for students to take the activity further if they complete it early. For example, in a math centre, students might solve a puzzle and then try creating their own version for a peer to solve.

Examples

Science (Mix and Flow of Matter)

- Experiment Station: Test solubility of various substances and record observations.
- Data Analysis: Analyze a prerecorded experiment's results and graph the data.
- Problem Solving: Solve a real-world scenario involving mixtures (e.g., water filtration).
- Concept Review: Match terms (e.g., viscosity, density) to their definitions and examples.

- Model Building: Create a diagram of particle movement in different states of matter.
- Discussion: Have a small-group discussion on environmental impacts of industrial mixtures.

Math (Ratios and Proportional Reasoning)

- Ratio Matching: Match word problems to their correct ratios.
- Scale Models: Use a scale to draw a simple map or object.
- Cooking Math: Adjust a recipe for a different number of servings.
- Word Problems: Solve ratio-related word problems.
- Creative Task: Create your own word problem involving ratios.
- Reflection: Discuss how ratios apply to real-life scenarios.

Social Studies (Canada: Governance and Rights)

- Charter Scenarios: Match scenarios to the correct section of the Charter of Rights and Freedoms.
- Debate Prep: Research and prepare arguments for or against a policy change.
- Timeline Building: Arrange key events in Canada's history of governance.
- Media Analysis: Analyze news articles for bias in reporting political issues.
- Policy Design: Draft a proposal for a new community policy.
- Reflection: Discuss connections between historical governance and current events.

ELA (Literary Analysis)

- Theme Hunt: Identify themes in short passages of text.
- Character Mapping: Create character maps for a chosen text.
- Device Detective: Identify literary devices in provided text excerpts.
- Writing Workshop: Draft and revise a short scene.
- Group Discussion: Discuss connections between the text and real-life issues.
- Creative Response: Create a visual representation of a key idea from the text.

Health (Stress Management and Wellness)

- Scenario Sorting: Match stress management techniques to scenarios.
- Mindfulness Station: Practice guided breathing or meditation using a provided script.
- Plan Creation: Design a daily wellness routine with focus on balance.
- Role Play: Act out strategies for resolving peer conflicts.
- Reflection: Write about how stress impacts students' personal lives.
- Research: Explore the benefits of physical activity for mental health.

Art (Exploring Style and Techniques)

- Style Matching: Match art pieces to their historical movements.
- Sketch Station: Sketch using a technique from a chosen artist.
- Media Exploration: Experiment with different art materials (e.g., charcoal, watercolor).
- Critique: Analyze a famous artwork using specific criteria.
- Collaborative Piece: Contribute to a group mural.
- Reflection: Discuss how art reflects societal values.

The Tool in Practice

In my English classroom, I used centres to support novel choice and enable myself to participate in book talks with my students. Students created book clubs of four to six classmates who were all reading the same novel. We began class with forty-five minutes of reading time and then spent the next forty-five minutes in centres. There were six centres, and the groups spent fifteen minutes at each one. That meant a full rotation took two classes. I saw my classes four times a week, so they worked at each station twice in a week.

Here were the centres:

Features of the Genre: While reading, each student selected a quote or a passage that demonstrated a feature of the genre for their novel. At the centre, they shared their passage and why they chose it, decided which one best exemplified the genre, and submitted the passage and their reasoning in point form using a provided graphic organizer.

Character Autopsy: Using a provided template, the group completed a character autopsy (detailing the character, with textual evidence). Each time they visited the centre, they had to choose a different character.

Literary Devices: Students completed a Google quiz on the literary terms that we had learned. The questions changed each time so that students were exposed to all the concepts and had to identify them in a variety of contexts.

Where in the World: Using paper, markers, and glue, students collaboratively built a model of the novel's setting. They used the provided tracking sheet to explain the choices they were making and connect them to evidence from the text.

Mind Map: Students identified one of the topics of the text and brainstormed evidence of that topic in the text.

Book Talk: The group conferenced with me to talk about the book.

Through their centre work, I was able to assess their reading comprehension in a variety of ways, and at the end of the novels, my students had a rich body of evidence to draw upon for their final analysis essays. Here are some samples of worksheets for a centre in language arts.

Features of the Genre – Group Graphic Organizer

Group Members and Novels:

Student	Novel

Genre of Our Novels: ____

Our Selected Quotes & Genre Features

Student	Quote or Passage (with page number)	Feature of the Genre Shown	Why This Matters

Our Group's Chosen Example

Highlight or star your group's BEST example. Why did we choose this one? (Give 2–3 strong reasons in point form.)

Pembroke Publishers © 2025 *Students in the Driver's Seat* by Erin Quinn and Tara Vandertoorn ISBN 978-1-55138-373-6

Character Autopsy

Task: You will complete an "autopsy" of one of the characters in your story.

Use the descriptions and questions below to guide you in conducting the autopsy.

1. HEAD — Intellectual side: What are the character's dreams?
2. HEART — Emotional side: What is your character's motivation? (Love, Pride, Peace, Justice Etc.…) What fears affect him/her? What does he/she love? Whom? How?
3. TORSO — Instinctive side: What doesn't he/she like about himself? What does he/she hide? What brings him/her pain? What does he/she fear?
4. LEGS — Right Leg: Strengths: What is one of your character's strengths? Left Leg: Weakness: What is one of your character's flaws?
5. FEET — Mobile side: Where has he/she been (literally and figuratively)? How has he/she been affected?
6. ARMS — Working side: How well does the character work with others in the story?
7. HANDS — Practical side: What conflicts does he/she deal with? How?
8. EARS — Hearing: What do others say about the character? How is he/she affected?
9. MOUTH — Communication: What are his beliefs? What song would symbolize his belief about life?
10 EYES — Seeing: What memorable sights affect him/her? What fears affect him/her? How?

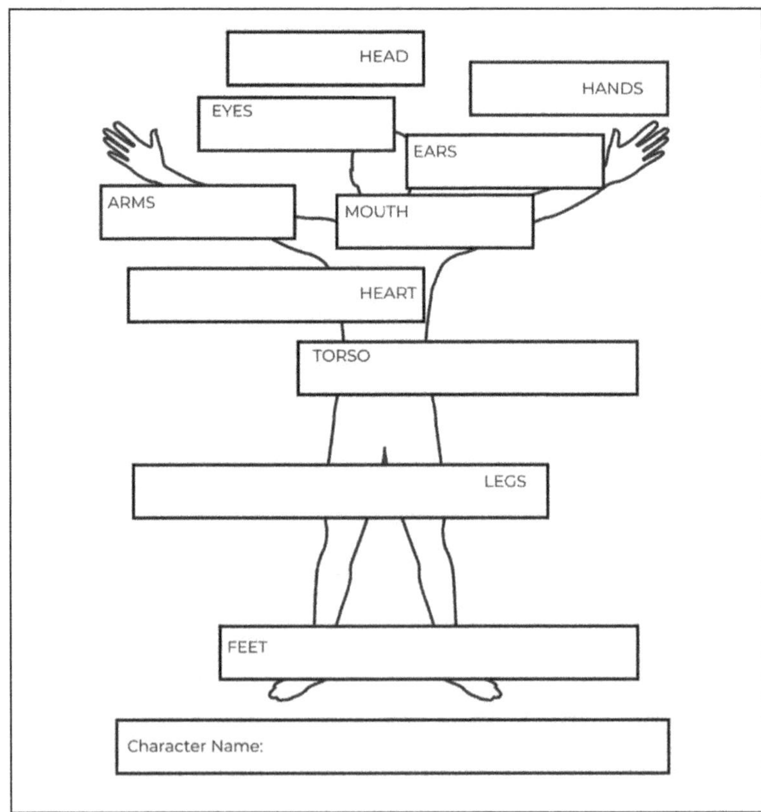

Where in the World

Purpose: Show your understanding of the novel's setting by building a model with your group.

What You're Doing

- Build a three-dimensional model of the novel's setting using paper, markers, and glue.
- Connect each part to evidence from the novel.

Things to Consider while You Work

- Where and when does the story take place?
- What descriptive details help you imagine the setting?
- What scenes or places are important to the plot?
- How does the setting affect the mood or characters?
- What parts of the setting should be included in your model?

Steps

1. Use your annotations for parts of the book that describe the setting.
2. Plan your model. Sketch a layout on the back of this sheet.
3. Build your setting using paper, markers, glue, and your creativity.
4. Explain what each part represents and include a detail or quote from the novel.

Element	Evidence	Explanation

Pembroke Publishers © 2025 *Students in the Driver's Seat* by Erin Quinn and Tara Vandertoorn ISBN 978-1-55138-373-6 

Mind Map

Instructions: Write one of the topics your books have in common in the centre box.
Then, work together to find evidence in your books of this topic. Write the evidence in the
surrounding boxes.

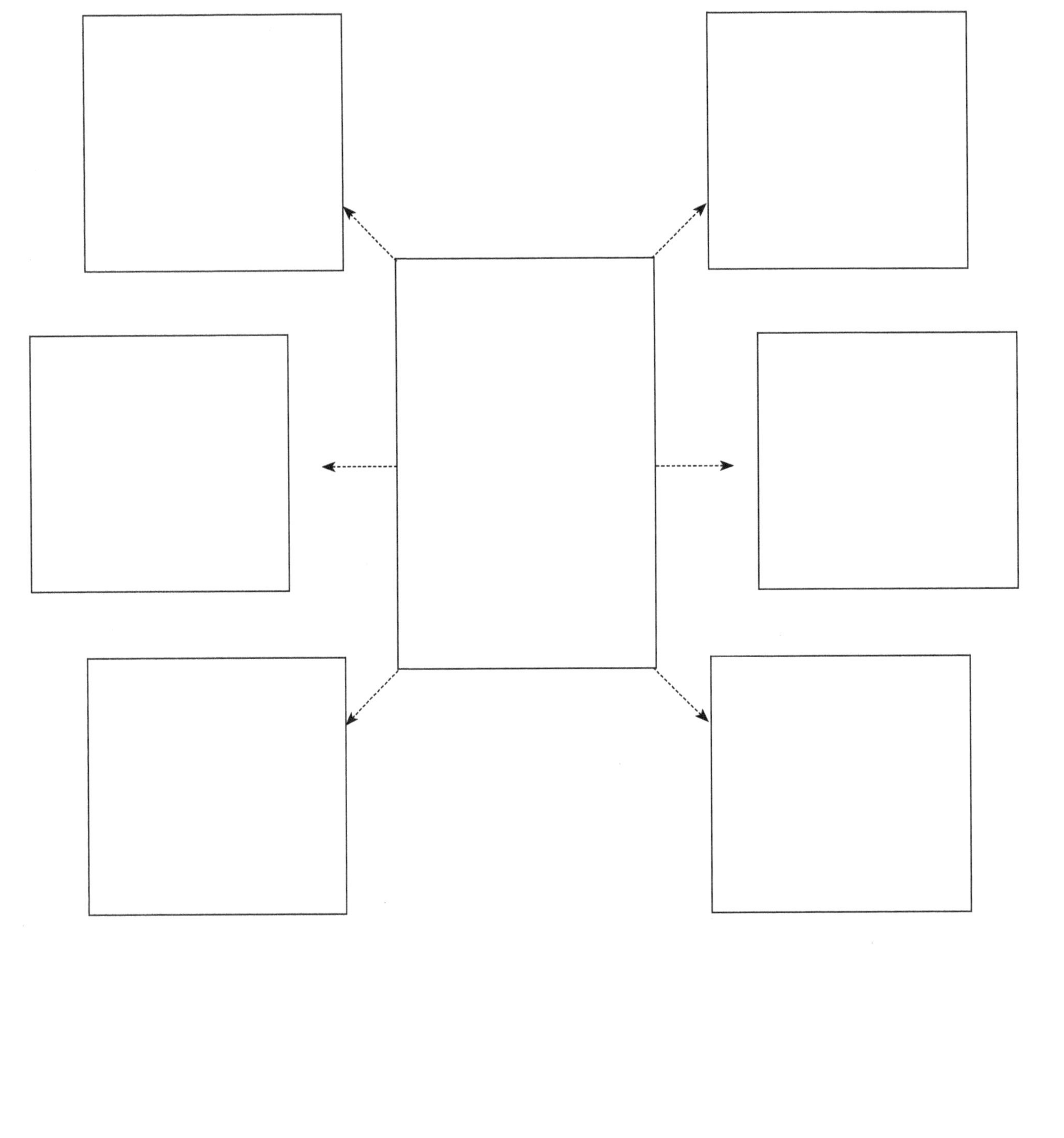

Book Talk Questions

Every so often, we're going to chat about your book and how it's going. If you have something specific you want to talk about, we can use your ideas. But if you're stuck for ideas, the following questions can support our discussion.

General Questions

- What made you choose this book?
- How's it going so far? Are you enjoying it?
- What's happening? What part are you at?
- Would you recommend this book to someone else? Why or why not?

Thinking Deeper

- What's a moment or scene that stood out to you so far? Why?
- How would you describe the main character? What do you like or dislike about them?
- What's a challenge or conflict the character is facing? How are they handling it?
- If you were in the character's shoes, what would you do differently?

Making Connections

- Can you connect this book to something else you've seen, read, or experienced?
- Can you relate to any of the characters or situations? How?
- How do the events in this book connect to something happening in the real world?

Looking Ahead or Reflecting

- What do you think might happen next?
- Is there anything you wish the author would do differently?
- If you could ask the author one question about the book, what would it be?

Choice Boards

What Is It?

Choice boards are tools that support students in making decisions about how to practice or demonstrate their learning of a specific concept. There are many different ways to set up choice boards, some of which we will review below. Typically, teachers set up choice boards with several columns, each of which represents a different skill, type of thinking, or depth of response. In each column, there will be several different options for tasks students can complete. Each student is then invited to choose a task in each column to complete.

Why Do It? Peeling Back the Pedagogy

The pedagogical reason for a choice board is in its name: choice. Choice boards can offer several advantages for both teachers and students. For people who aren't practiced at integrating choice into teaching and learning, choice boards can be an excellent way to dip their toes in. For some, the thought of offering free choice to students can be daunting. A choice board limits the amount of choice to several predefined options, which can be easier for teachers to manage. There may also be specific outcomes a teacher needs students to demonstrate their understanding of, and a choice board is a practical way to ensure students demonstrate all these different components, with each column of the choice board reflecting a different part.

Choice boards can be an excellent scaffold for students who might struggle to make decisions. A choice board can offer several possibilities to the student, and then the student can choose between them. Choosing well is a skill that must be developed, and choice boards can be a step towards more open choice. Sometimes students don't know what they don't know, and choice boards give students a starting point from which to choose.

How to Do It

There are many different purposes and iterations of choice boards. We will outline several possibilities below.

For Practice

Choice boards can be used as students are practicing a new skill. For example, when learning a new math concept, students can choose to work through a problem in a choice board. The headings of the choice board could be "Just the Facts," "Application," and "Word Problems," and students would be invited to choose one activity in each column to complete.

For Mastery

Following a unit to build a skill, students can apply what they know to show mastery of the concept. For example, perhaps your students have been learning different ways to create suspense in writing. The columns of your choice board may align with the strategies they have been learning about, such as "Dialogue," "Foreshadowing," and "Vocabulary." Students can choose a different culminating task in each column to show what they have learned about these different methods.

Organized by Strand

Many different disciplines incorporate different strands. For example, in language arts we often speak of the six strands: Reading, Listening, Viewing, Writing,

Speaking, and Representing. In math, we can organize around the five strands of mathematical proficiency: Conceptual Understanding, Procedural Fluency, Strategic Competence, Adaptive Reasoning, and Productive Disposition. In social studies, we could use the dimensions of historical thinking: Establish Historical Significance, Use Primary Sources, Identify Continuity and Change, Analyze Cause and Consequence, Take Historical Perspectives, and Understand the Ethics of Historical Interpretations. Other disciplines also involve different strands or themes. A choice board could be set up with each strand as a column, and students choose one activity from each column to demonstrate their understanding of a concept through each strand.

Organized by Complexity

A choice board could be organized by different levels of thinking to allow students to demonstrate their understanding of a topic. One way to do this is to use Bloom's Taxonomy as the columns of the choice board: Remember, Understand, Apply, Analyze, Evaluate, Create. The Depth of Knowledge (DOK) Levels are another way to organize by complexity Level 1 (Recall), Level 2 (Skill/Concept), Level 3 (Strategic Thinking), and Level 4 (Extended Thinking).

Organized by Topic

A choice board could be a way to assess your students' understanding of a variety of topics in a unit. For instance, you could invite students to choose one activity from each topic related to a study of each of the regions of Canada, where they must choose one activity in each column to show their understanding of all the regions.

Organized by Points

Another way to organize a choice board is to state the total number of points students must earn, assigning a point value to each task in the choice board. Students choose activities to complete in order to add up to a final point value. It would be up to each student to decide whether they wanted to complete several tasks worth lower point values or fewer, more complex tasks worth higher point values.

A Combination

Finally, you could combine two or more of these methods, such as using topics or strands to organize your columns and complexity of thinking to organize your rows. Then, you could instruct your learners to select tasks in a tic-tac-toe, ensuring they cover all the topics *and* are completing tasks in both low-level and higher-complexity thinking.

The Tool in Practice

My grade-nine students had been engaged in independent reading all semester. We had been working on deepening our understanding of how authors developed characters, advanced the plot, and used figurative language to create vivid imagery. At the end of this work, I wanted to assess my students' understanding of these concepts, so I developed a choice board for them to show what they knew.

On the next page you will see the choice board I made for them as they finished their most recent independent reading books. I explained to my students that I wanted them to choose one task from each column as their final project for their independent novel study.

Characterization	Plot	Literary Devices
Create a social media account for one of the characters in your book. Create at least three posts from your character, demonstrating your understanding of the character and how they change through the book. Use hashtags and interactions with other characters to show your understanding.	Create a plot diagram of the plot of your book. Be sure to label all the significant moments and turning points. You need to include the inciting incident, rising action, conflict, climax, and falling action.	Create a personal dictionary of at least ten literary terms and include examples from your novel of these terms. Include a short explanation of the effect of these literary devices in the novel.
Write a poem or song from the perspective of one of the characters in your novel, showing how they change through the book and what they are struggling with.	Create a metaphorical road map of the plot of your novel. Represent the inciting incident, rising action, conflict, climax, and falling action metaphorically through mapping components (consider scale, legend, labels, names/titles, etc.). Include an artist statement explaining your metaphors.	Create a Frayer model for ten of the literary devices we learned about. Give a definition, an example from your novel, a non-example, and include a drawing of each device.
Build a mind map showing your understanding of the major characters in your book. Use the branches in your mind map to show connections between characters, and explore how they grow and change in the story.	Write an alternative ending to your novel. If the conflict had not been resolved as it had, how would the story change? Include a short reflection after your story exploring how the climax and plot of your novel would change with the change in the conflict resolution.	Create a piece of artwork that incorporates five of the literary devices you noticed in your novel. Include a written artist statement exploring your choices.
Do a "character autopsy" — dissect a character, representing through drawing and words who they are, what they care about, how they are connected to other characters and things, what they struggle with, etc.	Create a new book cover for your novel, using artwork to represent key parts of the novel's plot. Include an artist statement exploring how your artwork reflects your novel's inciting incident, rising action, conflict, climax, and/or falling action.	Find five pages in your novel where you notice literary devices that create vivid imagery. Get your teacher to photocopy these pages for you. Then use these pages to create blackout poetry, using a marker to black out parts of the page you want to remove. The literary device should be included in the parts that remain. Write an artist statement for your five poems, exploring how the literary devices work to create imagery.

Write a well-structured analysis of your main character. In your essay, discuss what the character struggles with and how they change over the course of the novel. Be sure to incorporate your own personal connections and opinions.	Write a well-structured analysis of your novel's plot. In your essay, discuss the moves you noticed the author using to develop and advance the plot. Be sure to incorporate your own personal connections and opinions.	Write a well-structured analysis of your novel's figurative language. In your essay, discuss the language you noticed the author using to create vivid imagery and interest. Be sure to incorporate your own personal connections and opinions.
Propose your own project that demonstrates your understanding of your book's main character. Clear it with your teacher before you begin.	Propose your own project that demonstrates your understanding of your book's plot. Clear it with your teacher before you begin.	Propose your own project that demonstrates your understanding of your book's use of figurative language. Clear it with your teacher before you begin.

As I created the choice board, I thought about my students—what they enjoyed doing, what they found easier, and what they found more difficult. I thought about giving options for different kinds of kids—the ones who loved language arts and the ones who hated it. I considered including more traditional options such as essays, as well as more creative kinds of tasks such as a character autopsy. I was also purposeful in the last box in each column because I wanted my students to know that they could design a project if none of the listed options appealed to them.

Gamification and Game-like Learning

What Is It?

Gamification is the concept of applying game structures and components to learning. Essential to this idea is the fact that the structure of games is inherently fun to people, and that applying such structures can make learning feel like play. Closely related to gamification is the term "game-like learning." While gamification can mean adding game structures to traditional classroom processes, where game components like HP points can be earned by doing traditional classroom tasks like taking a multiple-choice quiz, game-like learning can be considered a more generous approach of incorporating game structures and strategies throughout the whole class, instructional design, and assessment practices. Game-like learning transforms the entire class into a game.

There are some common structures and processes you might see in a gamified classroom. Teamwork is one of the most common structures. Students might be working with a team to accomplish a goal or complete challenges. There is often some competition as well. Teams might be competing to earn the greatest number of points, or to earn resources to accomplish a task. Students or teams might select quests to participate in which might earn them resources or points. Side quests might add an added level of challenge as extension opportunities.

Why Do It? Peeling Back the Pedagogy

How does gamification promote student voice and choice? Choice is an essential part of games. When playing a game, there is always choice built in. Though there are set routines a player must follow when it is their turn, a player can decide what to do. This is true in gamification and game-like learning as well.

The now-defunct Institute of Play (2024) identified seven game-like learning principles to aspire to when designing game-like learning:

1. Everyone is a participant.
2. Failure is reframed as iteration.
3. Learning feels like play.
4. Learning happens by doing.
5. Feedback is immediate and ongoing.
6. Challenge is constant.
7. Everything is interconnected.

Each of these seven principles involves voice and choice. Student decision-making fuels game-like learning.

Most of all, it's fun. Incorporating game-like elements into the classroom creates engagement by making learning feel like fun.

How to Do It

When incorporating gamification or game-like learning into your class, you can start small or transform an entire unit of study. If starting small, you can use games to teach an isolated skill, such as card games to teach math concepts, or even use commercial games like Scattergories to work on language arts skills.

There is no one pathway to follow to develop games or incorporate game-like learning in your classroom. The best piece of advice we have is to play lots of games and think about how the mechanics could be incorporated into the classroom. As we have developed games for our students, this is where our best ideas have come from.

One area of caution when incorporating game elements in your classroom is around the idea of colonialism. Particularly when developing game-like learning around historical time periods or themes, it is easy to create a game where one culture is colonizing another. Be cautious of the implied messages in a game such as this. This consideration played itself out as we brainstormed ways we could make learning about the Spanish and Aztec conflict less about the Spanish conquering the Aztec and more about the differences in worldview that led to the end result of this conflict. Instead of making a game about the colonization, we instead developed a game where students were acting as secret agents to repatriate Aztec artefacts from around the world.

Some of the structures and mechanics you might consider incorporating into your classroom are:

Points, Currency, and Badges

When designing learning tasks, you might assign point values to each task. If students complete the task, they earn the points associated with it. Teachers can use points in different ways in their classroom. Some teachers create a competition where earning the most points is the goal. Other teachers allow students to use their points to spend on rewards or perks. And other teachers might have an ongoing game where points, or a currency like fake money, can be used in the game. Completing learning tasks then becomes the mechanism for playing the game. Points or currency can be used in the game to access certain tools, resources, or game mechanics.

Badges are another structure you can use. Earning badges can become a way of gaining prestige in the game or unlock special features for the player. Badges can also simply be about bragging rights — the more badges the student collects, the more bragging rights they have!

Quests

Reframing learning tasks as quests can provide an avenue for student choice. There is a lot of flexibility in how the quests are offered to your students. You might have different quests students can participate in with different rewards they can earn from each quest. Completing the quest earns them a reward, and the consequence for not completing the quest is that they will not earn the reward. This approach involves careful design on the teacher's part, as the teacher must consider what are the essential learning outcomes everyone must know and design the quests in a way to ensure that all students get the essential understandings. Another approach is to make all quests mandatory but allow teams to decide the order in which they complete them.

Side Quests

Side quests are a way you can build in extension for learners who are ready for it. You might be surprised at which students choose to do side quests. Students who love games are often quite motivated by them. We've had students take side quests home and complete them for homework even though they were not required.

Role Play and Story

Live action role play or tabletop role-play games like Dungeons & Dragons can serve as a flexible model for game-like learning in the classroom. Providing opportunities to use story and allow the students to determine how the story goes can be easily adapted to a range of curricular topics. In this approach, you can have students taking on the role of a character in the game and playing the game as this character.

Game Boards

Game boards can be adapted as a tool to move learning forward. Students can move along a game board, with each square presenting them with a task, challenge, or question to solve.

Cards and Dice

Cards are a part of many games in many different ways. You can have your students create cards for a game grounded in the content you are studying. You can have students earning cards, such as Pokemon or Magic: The Gathering, that give them special privileges. Multisided dice are another tool we have used often in our game-like learning in our classrooms. Dice can provide a moment of chance. As in Dungeons & Dragons, "Roll for it" has become a common phrase in our classrooms when students ask if they can do something in game-like learning situations.

The Tool in Practice

I was seriously stumped when I saw that my grade-five students had to learn about ancient civilizations in social studies. How on earth could I make Mesopotamia and ancient Iran relevant to them? As I looked for where these ancient civilizations showed up in pop culture, I found one place where they did appear: games. I had played the computer game *Civilization* when I was a kid, and I decided to develop a game for my students loosely based on the idea of ancient civilizations competing for dominance.

I created six fictional civilizations and organized my students into six corresponding groups in which they played for the entirety of the game. The goal of the game was to advance their society in geology, technology, governance, social structure, culture, and the military—components that made certain ancient civilizations stable. Then I developed quests around each of these components, designing learning tasks where students learned how different ancient civilizations made decisions within all these realms. In these quests, I incorporated learning games such as matching cards, escape room-style ciphers, puzzles, and word searches. Successfully completing each quest together earned the team a badge. I also incorporated an individual task where I could determine how well each student had learned the content by having them complete a graphic organizer or participate in a quick quiz. Each student earned coins for completing the individual tasks within the quest—the more thorough the understanding they demonstrated in their work, the more coins they earned. Earning a badge allowed the team access to a section of a civilization catalogue. Then they could pool their coins to purchase certain rewards in this section of the catalogue. For example, the group could purchase The Wheel, which meant their civilization had knowledge of wheeled transportation. The group could purchase Democracy, giving them access to this type of decision-making.

After they completed all the quests, the final stage of the game put all six civilizations head-to-head in physical and mental challenges where they could use the items they had purchased with their coins to their benefit. A group with wheeled transportation, for example, had access to wheels in the transportation challenge, where the task was to transport six heavy textbooks across the gym as quickly as possible using a collection of items.

Side quests and collaboration points were incorporated throughout the game, giving bonuses to teams who challenged themselves beyond the basics, and to teams who demonstrated excellent collaboration skills.

The best feedback I received from my experiment with game-like learning came from the students:

"We have to work hard today to get our badge!"

"Miss, is it time for social studies yet?"

"I'm going to take this side quest home so we can get the Irrigation Bonus!"

"We decided to pool our coins to buy the Written Word."

Every day of this game, my students used their understanding of ancient civilizations in a deeper way than they ever could have by learning through traditional methods.

Heat Mapping

What Is It?

Heat mapping is a decision-making tool borrowed from design thinking methods (see, for example, the *Design Thinking for Libraries Toolkit* developed by IDEO). Heat mapping is a quick way to see what ideas or opinions are most exciting or interesting to a group of people. It can help eliminate or narrow down ideas.

Heat mapping is a tool that is used after ideas are generated. It works very well as a step following the protocol of affinity mapping. Once ideas are generated, students are given a number of voting stickers. Round dot stickers that are easily found at a stationery store work well, but any kind of sticker works fine. Every student is then invited to vote for their top ideas generated in a brainstorming section. As the class looks at the "heat" created by the voting stickers, they can then eliminate ideas that have no or few votes, and focus on those ideas that have a lot of energy around them. This is also a great tool to use when you want students to vote for or rank ideas.

Why Do It? Peeling Back the Pedagogy

When engaging students in making choices in their learning, one of the common problems educators run into is how to create groups for projects. Do I put students in groups with friends? Do I group people interested in the same topic? Heat mapping is one way we can see what ideas or topics are exciting to a group of people. There are so many social and academic considerations when forming groups for projects. Heat mapping can help alleviate some of these concerns by identifying the topics that interest people.

There are good reasons why stickers are used as opposed to, say, having students highlight the ideas they like best or put their initials next to ideas they like. Having a tangible, finite "ballot" forces a couple of things to happen. If an educator gives each student three stickers to vote with, the student has to evaluate all the ideas. It forces each student to think critically about the ideas to determine which ones they might eliminate and only select the ideas they feel most strongly about. Sometimes there are so many great ideas that narrowing it down to three is very difficult. In other times, a clear favorite might emerge and selecting a second or third idea they like just as well might be more challenging. Requiring exactly three votes encourages critical thinking.

How to Do It

Materials
- An existing list of brainstormed ideas or topics
- Dot stickers or other stickers

Protocol
1. Distribute a predetermined number of voting stickers to each student. The number of votes is dependent on the size of the list of existing ideas and the amount of narrowing you need to do. A large list might necessitate five votes, where a smaller list could do with two or three.
2. Using your existing brainstormed list of topics or ideas on sticky notes or chart paper, invite students to vote for their favorites by sticking their dots on the appropriate notes or paper. Alternatively, you might vote for "most promising," "most doable," "most interesting," or "most original." The criteria or superlatives you give to students as a prompt depends on why you are using this protocol and what you wish to do with the ideas afterwards.
3. After everyone has voted, gather around the heat map and discuss the results of the vote.
4. Depending on the results of the vote, you might need to narrow the ideas down even further. In this case, you can remove the ideas that received no or few votes and give students another set of stickers in a different color to vote again. In this second vote, you would likely give students fewer stickers than the first vote to narrow the ideas down even further.

This tool can be used in a variety of settings for a variety of purposes. Most often, it is useful when working as a whole class to identify ideas or topics for a project. Perhaps a teacher wants to group her students for a project where they are choosing a topic to research or present about, but also wants to group her students based on interest. She might have the class generate ideas for the topics they could focus on in the project, and then use heat mapping to narrow down the list of topics to those the students in the class are most interested in. From here, she can offer the narrowed down list to them and have them rank their choices so you can assign them to like-minded groups.

Another reason this protocol might be used is if the class is trying to make a decision together. Of course, there are always good pedagogical reasons why doing something as a whole class is a good idea. This protocol can be a democratic way to see what the group prefers or is interested in. For example, perhaps the teacher wishes to engage the students in selecting a film to watch as a whole-class minilesson on what motivates characters. The class can brainstorm about films that have strong characters, and then the class can vote on which one they want to watch. The film with the most votes is the one the teacher will screen for the class.

The Tool in Practice

Everyone was clustered around our brainstorming wall, with large sheets of chart paper plastered over one wall in our classroom. Some students were sitting cross-legged at the front as others kneeled or stood behind them. I made my way through the group, handing each student a sheet of three dot stickers.

"Your job," I explained, "is to put your three stickers next to the ideas you like the best. These should be the three ideas you feel would make the best winter performance." We had spent the week brainstorming ideas for our class's performance at our winter concert.

As I passed out the last set of stickers to the final student, I told them they could go and put their stickers on the wall now. I watched as my students reviewed the options, reminding themselves of the discussions we'd had throughout the week. We had discussed audience and purpose and had used several brainstorming techniques to come up with the ideas for our nondenominational winter concert.

I noticed that Julio went straight for the first idea he had excitedly shared, a rap version of the song "Let it Snow." He put one of his stickers next to this idea. Then he carefully considered his remaining two stickers. He wandered over to the idea Alice had suggested on Wednesday, which was to perform a scene from *The Grinch Who Stole Christmas* but change it to *The Grinch Who Stole Winter*. He put a sticker beside this one. I watched Julio as he watched his classmates, looking to see what ideas they thought were exciting. There were many stickers beside "The Twelve Days of Winter" and lots beside Lewis's idea of an original play about a snowstorm that nearly prevented everyone from coming to the concert. Julio placed his final sticker on the latter.

Once everyone had voted, we all returned to our places gathered around the posters. It was easy to see where the heat in the room was. Our group loved the Grinch, and we also liked the idea of an original winter tale starring Shrek. The winter rap also got lots of votes.

"What if we combined a few of these ideas?" I said. "We could smash together the Grinch and the winter storm, and stir in a rap performance," I suggested. The kids beamed. In looking for the ideas that generated the most heat, we ended up finding an easy compromise which made everyone happy.

Heat map

Inventories

What Is It?

An inventory is a survey students can complete to brainstorm and articulate their habits and preferences. It can be a tool that looks back into the past, allowing students to reflect on their previous choices and experiences, and also looks into the future, with opportunities to reflect on what students might like to try, do, and experience. There are many kinds of inventories: reading inventories, writing inventories, topic inventories, and interest inventories.

Why Do It? Peeling Back the Pedagogy

Inventories allow students to reflect on their interests, habits, and preferences. They can be important tools in supporting students in making informed choices about their work, and choosing texts, topics, and forms that align with each student's personality. Many of the mentors we look up to use inventories to help them learn about their students (e.g., Atwell, 2007; Kittle, n.d.; Ripp, 2017).

One of the most important things we have learned after we purposefully focused on embedding voice and choice into our teaching practice is that when students are not used to being asked to make choices about their work in school, they might not necessarily know how. Students will often default to what they know — things they have previously done in school, projects they have done before, or texts they've previously read.

In our language arts work, we often give students the opportunity to design their own projects. At the beginning of the year, when we ask our students to choose their texts, some of them really struggle with this. Sometimes, we open it up and let them choose any kind of multimodal text that includes writing but can also involve speaking or visuals. There are so many possibilities of different kinds of texts students can choose that resonate with things that bring them joy. A magazine, a piece of art with an artist statement, a script for a movie they love, a manga series, or even an Instagram account can be a text they can choose. But so often students opt for texts that are familiar: *Diary of a Wimpy Kid*, *Harry Potter*, and *National Geographic* books. Inventories make gentle suggestions to help students think of possibilities outside of what they might typically consider.

Inventories can help students identify forms and genres they might work in, too. A student who is athletic might choose hockey as their topic. "I'll make a poster," the student often replies, when asked how they will represent their work, because making posters is something students do quite often in school. "Why? What for?" we ask. "Ummmm…for you?" they'll ask, uncertainly. "But I don't want a poster about Connor McDavid. Why would you make me a poster about Connor McDavid?" The conversation continues, with the student thinking about what kind of text she, as a hockey fan, might enjoy. Inventories can help identify possibilities beyond what a student might immediately imagine.

Inventories can also provide ways that students can identify possibilities for their work, and remind them of things that will truly bring them joy. They are also important in helping you learn more about the students you teach so you can target your instruction toward your students. Song analysis is something we often do with our students as an introduction to close reading and poetic devices, but when we learned our students *hate* Taylor Swift from the inventories we did with them, we chose a rap song instead as the song we analyzed together as a class.

How to Do It

The procedure for doing an inventory is quite simple.

1. Decide the format you will use, be it on paper or a digital form like Google Forms.
2. Think about the information that would be helpful for you and your students.
3. Administer your survey.
4. Review the results. Make the survey accessible to the student for them to use to inform their choices.

You can, of course, personalize your survey to suit your students and your context. Here are a few ideas for some questions you might ask that could be helpful.

Interest Inventory for Younger Students

Student Name: ____

What are your favorite things to do?

Do you take lessons or are you part of a team outside of school? Which ones?

What are your favorite books?

What do you like to watch on TV or online?

What do you like to listen to? Music, radio, podcasts? What are your favorites?

What does your family do on weekends or when you have time off together?

Interest Inventory for Older Students

Student Name: ____

If you could be doing anything in the world right now, what would you be doing?

What were some of your favorite things you did this summer?

What are your hobbies? What do you like to do when you have spare time?

What TV shows, movies, YouTube videos, etc. do you like to watch?

Who do you like to listen to? Musicians? Podcasts?

What do you like to read? (Novels, graphic novels, magazines, comics, webcomics, manga, etc.)

Are there creators you follow online? What do you like about them?

Who are your favorite celebrities?

Do you have any favorite brands?

Anything else you're really into?

Reading Inventory for Younger Students

Student Name: ____

Do you like to read?

   Yes   It Depends   Not really

Would you consider yourself a good, average, or bad reader?

   Good   Average   Bad

Why?

Would you say you are a slow, average, or fast reader?

   Slow   Average   Fast

What are your favorite books?

Are there other things you read that are not books? This could be magazines, online texts, or other media.

What do you want to improve in your reading this year?

Reading Inventory for Older Students

Student Name: ____

Do you like to read?

Yes	It Depends	Not really

Would you consider yourself a good, average, or bad reader?

Good	Average	Bad

Why?

Would you say you are a slow, average, or fast reader?

Slow	Average	Fast

What have been your favorite books you've ever read? This can be when you were a kid, too!

What genres do you typically choose? Circle as many as you want.

Realistic Fiction	Fantasy	Dystopia
Action/Adventure	Poetry	Sports
Suspense/Horror	Mystery	Graphic Novel
Historical Fiction	Nonfiction (Real)	Memoir
Romance	Other: _______________	

What do you like to read that is *not* in books? This could be magazines, websites, social media, newspapers, comics, etc.

How do you typically choose what to read?

What are your goals as a reader this year?

Writing/Form Inventory for Younger Students

What do you like best about writing?

What do you like least about writing?

Finish these sentences:

Writing is easy when…

Writing is hard when…

Would you consider yourself a good, average, or bad writer?

        Good   Average   Bad

Why?

Would you say you are a slow, average, or fast writer?

        Slow   Average   Fast

What do you like to write best? Circle as many as you like.

Stories	Information	Opinions
Comics/Graphic Novels	How-To	Diaries/Personal Stories

Other: ___________________

Writing is more than just using the alphabet. We can write in lots of different ways. Circle any of these other kinds of writing you enjoy.

Making art	Making crafts	Taking pictures
Making videos	Building stuff with LEGO or with blocks	Making things with wood or cardboard
Cooking food or baking	Making electronics like robots or building computers	Building digitally as with Minecraft
Sewing	Making music	Making audio (podcasts, recordings)
Interior design/decorating	Digital design (Canva, photoshop, etc.)	Making with your body (ex. dance, sports)

Anything else you like to make?

Writing/Form Inventory for Older Students

Do you consider yourself a writer?

      Yes   It Depends   Not really

Would you consider yourself a good, average, or bad writer?

      Good   Average   Bad

Why?

Would you say you are a slow, average, or fast writer?

      Slow   Average   Fast

Finish these sentences:

I write best when….

Writing is hard when…

Writing is easy when…

What do you like to write best? Circle as many as you like.

Stories   Information   Opinions

Comics/Graphic Novels   How-To   Diaries/Personal Stories

Other: ________________

Writing is more than just using the alphabet. It's representing your ideas and sharing them with others. Let's think now about other ways you like to write.

What kinds of audiovisual texts do you like to create (e.g., movies, videos, TikTok, Instagram reels, etc.)?

What kinds of audio texts do you like to create (e.g., songs, podcasts, recordings, etc.)?

What kinds of physical texts do you like to create (e.g., art, crafts, photography, woodworking, cooking, baking, sewing, robotics, etc.)?

Pembroke Publishers © 2025 *Students in the Driver's Seat* by Erin Quinn and Tara Vandertoorn ISBN 978-1-55138-373-6 

The Tool in Practice

One of the very first things I did with my fifth-grade class when I met them at the beginning of the school year was get them to complete a few different inventories. I usually spaced these out so the students were only completing one inventory each day for a few days in a row so I didn't overload them.

We started our very first day of school with a general survey asking some things about who the students were as human beings—what family they came from, who their friends were, and what kinds of things they liked to do. The second day, I gave them a reading inventory, to learn more about who they were as readers. On the third day, I wanted to ask them about writing. I asked this week's Paper Pusher, Fiona, to hand these sheets out.

As she placed a paper on each student's desk, I explained the task. "Today, I want to know more about the things you like to create. We're going to write lots and lots this year. But it might not always be the kind of writing you might be used to. We won't always be writing with a pencil to paper, though we definitely were going to do lots of that. There's lots of different ways to write because writing means coming up with and communicating your ideas.

"That's why you'll notice that on this survey, I'm asking you about different ways you like to create. Chefs write through the food they create. Musicians write through the songs they compose. Artists write through the artworks they paint. All of these are very valid ways to write. Let's take some time now to answer the questions. Please take out a pencil and get started. If you're confused by any of the questions, come sit with me at the horseshoe table and I'll help you."

I went and sat at the horseshoe table, and a few students joined me right away for some extra support. I helped Sierra work through the questions. I read them to her, and she wrote her answers as follows.

In conversation with Sierra as she completed her inventory, I learned that she loved to write and create, but sometimes the need for conventionality in her writing had prevented her from feeling joy in that creativity. I also learned that she had a great talent for building with her hands and felt most joyful when she was using her imagination to invent stories and ideas in her treehouse in her backyard. This gave me important information about where to begin with her, as well as how to help her navigate the parts of writing she disliked, like spelling and editing. I never would have known these things if I hadn't asked.

Writing/Form Inventory

What do you like best about writing?
I like coming up with stories.

What do you like least about writing?
I'm bad at spelling and always forget capitals and periods.

Finish these sentences:

Writing is easy when…
I'm allowed to write about whatever I want.

Writing is hard when…
I have to write about an idea my teacher picks.

Would you consider yourself a good, average, or bad writer?

Good   Average   (Bad)

Why?
Because I'm kind of bad at spelling.

Would you say you are a slow, average, or fast writer?

(Slow)   Average   Fast

What do you like to write best? Circle as many as you like.

(Stories)   Information   (Opinions)
(Comics/Graphic Novels)   How-To   (Diaries/Personal Stories)
Other: _________________

Writing is more than just using the alphabet. We can write in lots of different ways. Circle any of these other kinds of writing you enjoy.

(Making art)   (Making crafts)   Taking pictures

(Making videos)   (Building stuff with LEGO or   (Making things with wood or
                       with blocks)   cardboard)

Cooking food or   Making electronics like robots   (Building digitally as with
baking   or building computers   Minecraft)

Sewing   Making music   Making audio (podcasts,
                                                 recordings)

Interior design/   Digital design (Canva,   Making with your body (ex.
decorating   photoshop, etc.)   dance, sports)

Anything else you like to make?
I have a treehouse in my backyard and I like to play there with my sister and make pretend food out of like leaves and berries and stuff, and decorate my treehouse with nature things.

Synthesizing Learner Outcomes

What Is It?

One of the most powerful ways teachers can identify opportunities for incorporating more voice and choice into their classroom is by taking a serious look at the learner outcomes in their program of studies or standards. This work should be done first by the teacher and then with students. Oftentimes students ask us, "Why do I need to know this?" because the standards we are beholden to in our programs of study, standards, or curriculum are a mystery to students.

In many places, programs of study standards are often very lengthy documents written in "teacher language." By engaging in a process where the teacher looks for ways to condense and synthesize the program of study, teachers can free up their time to achieve outcomes in efficient ways, which lets both teacher and student focus on spending their time on what's most important.

Posting a learner outcome or target for students is a common practice, but what if we invited students to interact with learner outcomes in a more meaningful way? This protocol invites students to treat learner outcomes as loose parts and find ways to organize them in interesting, surprising, and original ways.

Why Do It? Peeling Back the Pedagogy

Being able to manipulate outcomes as loose parts communicates something subtle but important: that there are multiple pathways to achieving these learner outcomes. Architect Simon Nicolson introduced the concept of loose parts in the 1970s, originally as a concept in playground design. Early childhood educators and those inspired by the Reggio Emilia approach will be well familiar with loose parts. Angela Stockman (2016) has taught us important connections between loose parts and writing as well. The theory of loose parts invites students into the design space by providing them with different kinds of parts that can be arranged, manipulated, and configured in many different ways, opening up infinite combinations and permutations of creative ideas.

There are two parts to this protocol: the teacher part and the student part. Sometimes, it's easy for teachers to lose sight of what they are *actually* required to teach. For example, does your English language arts curriculum actually require you to teach students to write a five-paragraph essay? Or does it ask students to analyze and write persuasively? Does it require you to teach short stories? Or does it require students to learn the elements of story? These important distinctions can allow for much more creativity and much more relevant resources and learning activities for your students.

Once we as teachers have taken a critical look at our learner outcomes, we can invite students to do so too. When we invite students to interact in tangible ways with the learner outcomes we are required to teach, students gain a much deeper understanding of what they need to learn, and then we can move on to how they might learn it. The richness of teaching really resides in the *how*, and this is where student voice and choice live, too. In most places, our government or district decides what needs to be taught, but how we teach these outcomes is up to us.

How to Do It

1. Print your program of study or standards. Be sure to print single-sided, not double-sided.

2. Cut out the outcomes so each outcome is on a separate piece of paper.
3. Now, play! Clear a large space on a table or wall. Move the outcomes around. Group "like" ideas. Look for points of conversion: Are there several outcomes that are essentially saying the same thing? Or outcomes where you might be looking at a similar process but in different kinds of texts or through different kinds of content?
4. The next step is to look for opportunities for synthesis. Can the groupings be summarized in a short sentence or two?

When engaging in this activity with students, it may be overwhelming to present them with the entire program of study all at once. Teachers may find it more helpful to give students only certain parts of the curriculum or to engage in some synthesis before giving these synthesized outcomes to students.

The Tool in Practice

I handed each student a playing card as they entered the room. Each of my desks had a corresponding card, and this was where they would sit today. My desks were clustered in six groups of five that day because we were going to collaborate.

In my hands, I held six envelopes.

"Today, we're going to take a look at our language arts curriculum. Our government decides what we need to learn, but it's our job to figure out how. In these envelopes, I've cut up all the things we have to learn this year. Your job is to work together with your group to sort them. We're going to sort them in lots of different ways today. Let's start by sorting them in whatever way makes sense to you first." I handed an envelope to each table group.

Each group opened the envelope, pulling out little strips of paper. I had written out the curricular objectives for our language arts curriculum as "I can" statements and simplified the language a bit so my ninth graders could understand. I hadn't included every single outcome – I'd prioritized the outcomes that were essential and left out some minor ones that I knew we could tackle in very specific situations.

I wandered around the room and watched as the students read the statements aloud and discussed how to group them. I placed a stack of sticky notes and a marker on each group's table for them to label their categories.

"I can identify the theme in a story," Caleb read.

"We can put that over here, beside these ones that have to do with finding a deeper meaning," Kingston suggested.

"Yup. Do we think this one, 'I can create a theme in a story,' should also go over there?" Caleb asked.

"Hmm. Yeah, I think so," said Sage. "They're all about theme. Identifying and making your own." She wrote the word *THEME* in block letters on a sticky note and stuck it on the table above this cluster of outcomes.

After they finished their first round of sorting, I asked each group to share a little bit with the class about how they had sorted the outcomes. They shared lots of logical ways they found connections between the outcomes.

"Okay, now I want you to see if you can sort them into the six strands of language arts," I said. "Reading, listening, viewing, writing, speaking, and representing. Write those on sticky notes. Now, move the strips of paper to the side of your desk and start again." The students started moving around the strips of paper again. Pretty quickly, they got stuck.

Damian called me over to his group. "This doesn't work. Look: This outcome is 'I can express an opinion and support it with details.' I can do that when I'm writing *or* speaking. I can't put that in just one category."

"Oh, interesting," I said, playing along, pretending this wasn't my intention. "Can you share an opinion through representing too? Like, could an artwork present an opinion?"

"Yeah, definitely. Artists share opinions all the time. So I guess it could fit in three categories."

I let the students struggle through a bit longer before I called for them to stop, and we discussed this important realization: Reading and writing are more than just print. By playing with these outcomes as loose parts, my students realized that it was more about thinking than it was about form. We could read through many kinds of texts, and we could write in many ways that weren't just print. Below is a sample of what students realized about their learning after synthesizing their ideas.

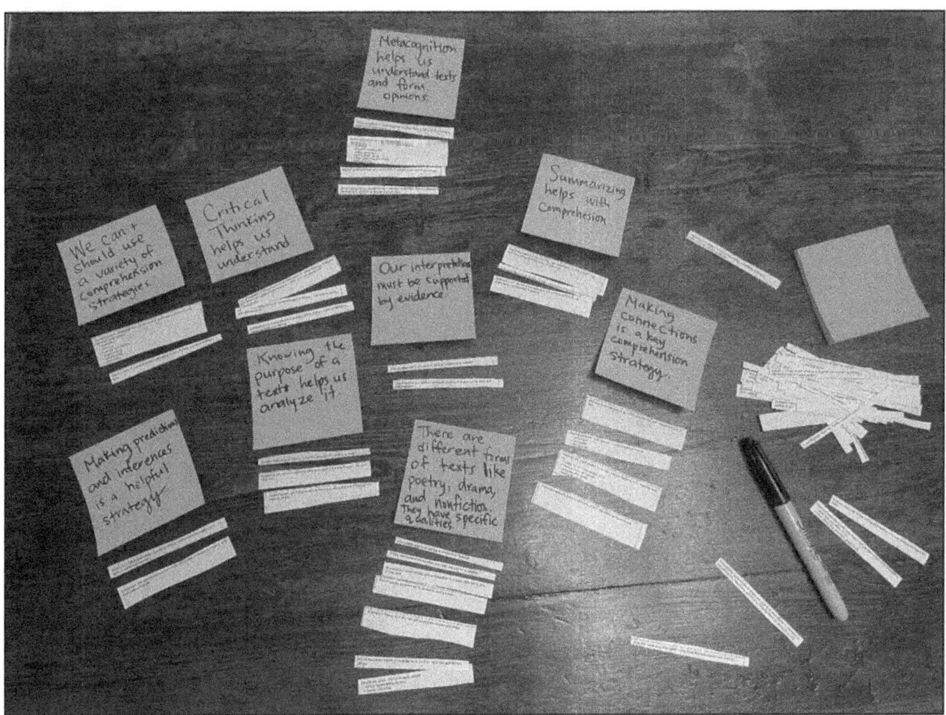

Live Drafts

What Is It?

Sports are an easy way to connect with many students in our classes. Even Tara, whose favorite sport is Theatresports™, can get on board with this tool. Most major sports franchise select players through a process called a draft. This is when each team takes turns choosing a player, from the available pool of players. A live draft is an excellent option to support students in self-selection while also ensuring variety across the class or grade. The teacher provides a predetermined list of options and individuals or groups make their choices in real time, similar to a sports team drafting players. There are a lot of possible ways to make this happen but the key is that the students are making the choice. This concept was refined collaboratively during the time we worked with Natasha Mueller Ruzycki and Ryan Molyneux.

Why Do It? Peeling Back the Pedagogy

The benefits of choice in increasing engagement are well-documented across a variety of subjects and grade levels. It is also worth noting that too much choice can be overwhelming. Iyengar and Lepper (2000) observe that performance and satisfaction actually increase when students are presented with fewer options. Balancing these two ideas is addressed with this tool as it is an effective strategy to support student choice with a large option set.

If students have the opportunity to contribute to the choices, it helps them become more risk-positive in idea generation as they are not beholden to the options they generate. Including teacher options can support students in envisioning options they hadn't considered and in meeting specific curricular outcomes.

How to Do It

There are a lot of possibilities with this simple tool!

1. Explain the assignment or task and review the success criteria.
2. Generate a list of possible topics. It is best to have more options than you need so that there is an authentic choice for everyone. Otherwise, the student or group to choose last is left with the only remaining choice. All options should also be high-quality and viable for the task. AI can be a great support in generating your topic options but should always be checked for accuracy. You can also brainstorm the options as a class or invite student input into the choices.
3. For longer or more complex tasks or for group tasks, have the students select three to five options from the list and identify the pros and cons of each option. They can then rank their choices in preparation for the draft.
4. The draft can take place several ways, with technology or without, but the basic method is that all students select their topic "live" so that by the end of the draft everyone has a topic.

Options

1. Use a shared document and have multiple classes making their choices, live, at the same time. The teacher can control the inputs or the students can have access as well. When an option is taken students must be prepared with their next choice. The process is full of chaotic enthusiasm and works best for low-stakes tasks or when all the options have similar value.
2. Students can earn their draft position based on a set of predetermined factors. For example, performance on background knowledge tasks can earn draft points or contributions to the classroom community can be tallied leading up to the draft. Just make sure that you view your choice through the equity lens to ensure that all students have access to earning the top draft position.
3. If the chaos of everyone calling out at once is not for you or your students, you can randomly select positions. It can be fun if students are allowed to trade, just as in a real draft. For example, a group that goes first but has two equally preferred options might trade their choice with a later group for future consideration.

The Tool in Practice

My eighth-grade students were creating a cross-curricular project that connected their core subjects. I taught two classes of humanities (English language arts and social studies), while my partner taught the same group for math and science. Together, we had been exploring the theme of "Innovators across Time."

We began with a conversation about the Renaissance and its impact on Western worldview, focusing on scientists, inventors, and mathematicians who changed how people thought about the world. Students noticed a glaring absence in these figures: diversity. To bridge this gap, we spent a class researching modern innovators—trailblazers in science, technology, engineering, and math who had defied odds and barriers. By the end of the period, students had compiled a list of more than 100 names, including people like computer scientist Timnit Gebru, inventor Granville Woods, and aerospace engineer Lonnie Johnson, to include in their draft picks for their class team.

We reviewed the list as a class, with students sharing a brief explanation about the people they had added to the list. Students were awarded "draft points" for connecting the "big ideas" of the Renaissance (imperialism, humanism, individualism, rationalism, etc.) to the people added to our list. We then reviewed the assignment (to write a biography and create a "player card" for a hallway Innovators Gallery) and the assessment criteria. Finally, students created a ranking of their top five choices to prepare for the draft and we broke any ties in draft points with the roll of a die (highest roll wins).

We used live drafts often in our classes, so it was at this point that some students traded positions for future considerations. For example, a student who had a less popular first choice traded their third place with a fourteenth-place student in exchange for a future up move. I didn't keep track of these deals and they were all done on the honor system. The next day we drafted!

As we approached the draft time, I started the countdown clock and opened up the Excel sheet on our SMART Board. Students were talking about the relative merits of the choices, with some trying to convince others to change their ranking. One student called out, "Hey, Miss, if you were drafting would you choose Mae Jamison or Katherine Johnson?" Another whispered, "Don't tell anyone but I found a really good source for Granville Woods, so I'm making him my second choice."

"If someone else gets him will you share your source?" I questioned.

"Of course," she replied. We were one minute away from beginning, so I called for everyone's attention.

"Welcome to our live draft! In a few moments, the list of possible choices will be going live. Both classes will be selecting a person at the same time and there can be no duplicates! You must be ready to make a choice when it's your turn or I will go to the next person. You will go in the order determined by your earned draft points. Are you ready?"

The energy in the class was palpable as we began the draft. There were cheers and calls of disappointment as names were selected. I could hear the banter from my partner class across the hall as well. When the last person had chosen, there were several names left over, so I asked, "Is there anyone who's unhappy with their choice and would like to switch for an unclaimed name?" There were no takers in my room, but I saw a switch happen on the live document from the other class.

"Okay! Let's get started with our research!"

Trailblazers	Class	Team
Timnit Gebru	85	Aisha, Mateo,
Fei-Fei Li	85	Liam, Aria,
Joy Buolamwini	84	Jamal, Saanvi,
Ayah Bdeir	83	Diego, Hana,
Alan Emtage	83	Noor, Elijah,
Juan Gilbert	84	Yuna, Marcus,
Akshaya Dinesh	83	Fatima, Luca,
Abinaya Dinesh	83	Neha, Isaiah,
Granville T. Woods	85	Amina, Kai,
Lonnie Johnson	83	Darius, Mei,
Aisha Bowe	83	Ravi, Leila,
Christina Roki	85	Keisha, Minh,
Sylvia Acevedo	84	Andres, Zahra,
Marc Hannah	85	Mila, Raj,
Gerald A. Lawson	85	Omar, Kiara,
Marie M. Daly	84	Santiago, Priya,
Patricia Bath	85	Niko, Alejandra,
Katherine Johnson	85	Tariq, Chloe,
Mae Jemison	85	Sofia, Jayden,
Gitanjali Rao	84	Anya, Jalen,
George Carruthers	84	Zain, Naomi,
Alice Augusta Ball	85	Carmen, Yusuf,
Euphemia Lofton Haynes	84	Kaito, Amara,
David Blackwell	84	Isla, Tariq,
Keren Skariah	84	Kwame, Lila,
Shirley Ann Jackson	83	Tenzin, Zara,
Herman Chinery-Hesse	84	Malik, Imani,
Marian Rogers Croak	84	Talia, Jun,
Elijah McCoy	83	Yaretzi, Amir,
Marie Van Brittan Brown	83	Vivaan, Lucia,

Sample Innovators live draft

Whole-Class Activities to Build Transfer Skills

What Is It?

There are a lot of opportunities in a class period to incorporate choice and encourage students to share their voices. What we like to do is think about how to build this into everyday moments so that we can develop skills in low-stakes, low-risk situations that can then transfer to larger projects with higher stakes, where students are more willing to take academic risks.

This is particularly relevant as students learn how to develop and express an opinion. Using music is a great gateway drug to poetry and engages students with a mode that reflects their culture and can also expand their perspectives. Making "Would you rather?" style choices helps students immediately express an opinion and conversations around the choices can invite the use of evidence and invite more nuanced thinking. Attendance questions are another way to support the sharing of opinions and can also serve as quick well-being checks.

Why Do It? Peeling Back the Pedagogy

The ability to transfer skills requires examples from multiple contexts and repeated opportunities to practice and apply the learning. The deeper, underlying structures should be explicitly identified to enable application to other situations. The key with activities like these is to keep the focus on the process.

In their work to promote and support the implementation of initiatives to foster the development of transferable skills in education systems across Latin America and the Caribbean, UNICEF (2021) identified twelve transferable skills: creativity, critical thinking, problem solving, cooperation, negotiation, decision making, self-management, resilience, communication, respect for diversity, empathy, and participation. While these initiatives focused on creating access, engagement, and equity in Latin American and Caribbean education contexts, the work is solidly grounded in current pedagogy. Identifying the skill and the way to develop and use it will support students in transferring these skills to new and unfamiliar contexts.

When students are motivated by the topic, motivated to learn, have previous knowledge on the topic, and can connect new to existing information then the transfer of learning can occur. We must model this and make it a conscious process for students.

How to Do It

Jam or not a Jam: Stating an Opinion with Song or Poetry

This is a great warmup to expressing a preference and you can slowly build up to asking for reasoning and evidence as students become more comfortable with the risk-taking that expressing a personal preference represents. Borrowed from a segment that CBC Music did on YouTube years ago, Jam or Not a Jam is on the surface a simple way for students to express an opinion. On the videos from CBC Music, the hosts would play a song for celebrities to listen to and the celebrity would determine if the song was a "Jam" — a good song, or "Not a Jam" — not a great tune. There are a lot of different ways that this type of activity can work in a classroom; here's one.

Play a song while students are coming into the classroom at the beginning of the day or after recess or lunch. Create a voting system. You can use magnets with student names on them and areas on a white board labelled "Jam" and "Not a Jam." You could use baskets with rocks with student names on them and two baskets labelled "Jam" and "Not a Jam." This could also be done digitally through a variety of online polling or voting software. As students listen to the song, they move their name to the category that best represents their opinion of the song they're hearing. This is a great way to begin class if you set the expectation that by the time the song is over, everyone has what they need to begin the day's learning and you have visually completed attendance. Any unmoved names represent absent students. You can also ask students to verbally share their opinion with a reason for it. Not all students need to share every day. In an English class, you can invite students to respond to specific questions that build literary analysis skills and use direct textual evidence from the song to support their ideas. This repeated practice with immediate feedback builds competency and transferability.

This or That

This is a classic take on the "Would you rather?" game. Ask students a question that requires a choice (this or that) and have them stand on the side of the room that corresponds with their choice. These types of questions can be lighthearted or serious, unrelated or relevant. In math, students can be asked to use math to justify their choice, extending the activity into an application of problem-solving and reasoning. Having students get up and move provides a movement break and allows for conversations related to their choices. Some examples are:

- Iced coffee on a snowy day or hot coffee in a heatwave?
- Sandals or Crocs?
- Toe socks or toe rings?
- Burping or farting?
- Float in freshwater or saltwater?
- Become an astronaut or an engineer?
- Become a doctor or a scientist?
- Thirty minutes of TV a day or four hours only on weekends?

Attendance Questions

These are questions that you ask as you take attendance. Start with low-risk, informational questions that help you get to know your students and give them the opportunity to become more comfortable with sharing. Some examples include favorite color, only child or sibling, hometown. You can then move into personal preference questions — dogs or cats, yes or no to pineapple on pizza, flip-flops or slides. You will know your students but we are often surprised when students assign a high-risk value to something we thought was a low-risk question. This usually looks like an unwillingness to engage with the question. Watch out for those questions that hide markers of status or class (favorite clothing brand, greatest all-time band, best holiday) as they are often high-risk questions for students who fear being judged by their peers.

Once you have built a community where students feel comfortable sharing, you can begin to ask more challenging questions. These can be connected to a concept or subject. For example,

- Who is your favorite character so far in the book we're reading?
- What moment or quote has stood out to you from the reading?
- Share a fact about freshwater.

Questions can also be connected to a skill:

- Solve a mental math question.
- Define a literary device.
- Name something that lives in saltwater.

One of our favorite ways to use this is to have the first name that we call identify a term, the next person defines it, and the next person provides an example. Remember, you don't always have to go down your classlist in the same order.

These types of activities can be a great way to gather additional assessment data as they allow you an opportunity to see students using their skills in a variety of contexts. For example, you can track the use of textual evidence to support analysis in students' responses over the course of a month or use a quick-response exit ticket to gauge understanding. Lots of these tools can also be used simultaneously.

The Tool in Practice

We began every class with a song. I played the song and video as students arrived. The agenda for that day's class was on the board so that everyone knew what we would be doing and could be ready with what they would need for our first task. That day, we were continuing our individual novel study, so by the time the song was over, everyone should have their book out, with a pencil and sticky notes, and be reading or annotating their text. Students who were using the audiobook for support were given a laptop and headphones. I was at the door greeting students as "What a Wonderful World" by Louis Armstrong played, with a video that featured scenes from the film *Good Morning, Vietnam.*

"Good morning," I said to the students as they entered the room. "As you move your 'Jam' or 'not' magnet, pay attention to this song and video. We are going to talk about juxtaposition today. Make sure you are ready to read by the time the song is over."

The song ended and I allowed everyone to quietly begin reading while I completed attendance and helped settle a few stragglers.

"Good morning everyone. If you could finish off your paragraph or page, I'd like your attention for a moment. Please flip to your terms and definitions in your notes and add 'juxtaposition.' Does anyone know this term already, from a previous class?" No hands were raised, so I wrote the definition on the board: *Two opposite elements close together or side by side in order to compare/contrast the two to show similarities or differences.* "Now, considering the song and video we just saw, where did you see juxtaposition?"

Several hands were raised and I called on Omar. "So, like, the guy."

"Armstrong," Cherie interrupted.

"Right. Armstrong is singing about how great the world is but the video shows all these pictures of war."

"Great. So the lyrics are juxtaposed with the images," I restated, making sure to emphasize the correct use of the vocabulary. "Why?"

"Well, I think that the juxtaposition makes you really think about whether the world is wonderful or not. It makes the violence seem kind of pointless, you know?" David suggested. I nodded and smiled at his use of the new term.

After a few more moments of discussion, I asked the students to pay attention to examples of juxtaposition in their own reading that day and make an annotation that identified the device and its purpose for their exit ticket that day.

At the end of class, I collected their sticky note annotations. I noted the names of a couple of students I would check in with the next day to clarify their understanding.

Self-Directed Minilessons

What Is It?

A minilesson is exactly what it sounds like: a short (ten minutes or less) lesson that targets one key concept or skill. To be most effective it should have a clear explanation and example with an opportunity to immediately practice the skill or concept. Minilessons work best when they are directly connected to the work that the student is doing at that moment. This direct connection or immediate opportunity to apply the learning is key. It is why grammar or spelling bell-ringer type lessons rarely translate to better writing (Pezzetti, 2018). Having a bank of minilessons accessible to students supports them in gaining the skills and knowledge they need when engaged in self-selected or codesigned projects or work. This approach can be particularly helpful if you have students making choices in terms of a genre or form they are working in. For example, perhaps you have students working on creating characters, but invite them to choose what form to do this in, such as a short story, a comic, a script for a film, a video game, or a fictional podcast. Self-directed minilessons can provide students with self-serve instruction in each of these genres and how characters are developed in each form. Minilessons can also support students in specific skills such as capitalization rules, solving a quadratic equation, or following the scientific method.

Minilessons can take any format that is helpful for your students and in your repertoire of tools to create with. For instance, a minilesson could be teacher-directed or it could be a slide deck, a video, or even a document. These tools can be accessed digitally or printed. Consider how the minilesson can be easily accessible for students to grab when needed. Digitally, they can be housed in Google Classroom or whatever learning management system your school district uses. If printed, a milk crate with file folders works well. We've also seen a genius idea online where a teacher used a shoe pocket chart and hung it on the wall and placed quarter page-size reference sheets in each pocket for the students to access when needed. If minilessons are teacher-directed, they should be carefully planned to ensure that they directly relate to the immediate work of the students participating.

Often, minilessons created by others can be found online. YouTube videos, websites, and other sources can be provided to students to support them in their task. Other times, you will need to create minilessons for your particular students.

Why Do It? Peeling Back the Pedagogy

One of the big shifts in thinking that we experienced when we opened up our teaching practice to prioritizing student voice and choice is the idea that there are more teachers than just you at the front of the room. Resources can be teachers. By providing an access point for students to find what they need, you are building independence in your students to find and use the tools they need in order to be successful. Of course, independence in this area needs to be scaffolded, and students need to be supported in identifying the need for a tool at a particular time. Over time and with practice, students of any age can do this independently when the minilessons are tailored to them.

How to Do It

1. Consider the context for your minilesson. You need to determine if the purpose of the minilesson is to help students learn and apply skills, apply a concept to different forms or genres, or something else. Considering what choices your students will be making in the task is helpful in considering what kind of minilesson will support them in achieving their goal.
2. Decide if you will look for preexisting resources online or if you will create the minilesson. Oftentimes, teachers already have the bones of a minilesson, and it's just the format of the lesson that needs to be adapted to make it possible for students to access it independently.
3. If choosing premade minilessons, make them accessible to students, either digitally or by printing them. Be sure to label them in a way that can support students in finding what they need quickly and easily.
4. If creating minilessons yourself, decide on a format (document, slide deck, video, or other). Finally, create the minilessons. We have found AI tools to be quite helpful in designing minilessons.

The Tool in Practice

While you can easily create your own minilessons, there are only so many hours in a teacher's day and there are many examples of this protocol in practice online. Khan Academy is a classic go-to resource for minilessons on a wide range of topics. It has many video tutorials as well as practice exercises students can do, related to many different curricular topics. A potential drawback of this source is that it is American and focuses on American curricula only.

We have some other favorite resources for online minilessons. Rebekah O'Dell is a master at video minilessons on her YouTube channel Mini Moves for Writers. Appropriate for teaching writing at middle- and high-school levels, O'Dell's video lessons each highlight a "move" she identifies in mentor texts she reads. Brian Tolentino is another YouTuber who creates video lessons for middle- and high-school writers.

Sample Self-Directed Minilessons

As mentioned, AI can be a time-saving tool to help you create a lot of personalized minilessons quickly. We will share a few minilessons we created with the help of AI. As you read through each minilesson we created to help students develop compelling characters across different genres, you might notice that many of the tips for creating compelling characters are genre-agnostic; lots of the suggestions are the same whether students are writing a story or creating a video game. However, the language and ways to communicate a sense of each character vary based on the genre, and these minilessons are a scaffold to help students translate common ideas about characterization to the particular genre they are working in. We highlight this use of AI to support your practice as it is a time-efficient way to ensure your students get the same core focus of your minilessons, which should align with the program of studies or standards your students need to master but are personalized and targeted towards whatever task they are completing.

On the following pages you will find sample minilessons you can print or make available online.

Let's Dive into Creating Awesome Characters for Your Short Story!

We're going to talk about something super important when it comes to writing a great short story – creating awesome characters that readers will love. Characters are like the heart of your story, so let's learn how to make them really stand out on the page.

1. **Get to Know Your Characters:** Before you start writing, take some time to think about who your characters are. What are their personalities like? Where do they come from? What do they want? Creating character profiles can help you get to know your characters better.

2. **Show, Don't Tell:** Instead of just telling your readers what your characters are like, show it through their actions, dialogue, and how they interact with others. For example, instead of saying, "Sara is brave," show Sara doing something brave that makes us see her courage in action.

3. **Use Specific Details:** Make your characters come alive by using specific details to describe them. Instead of saying, "She wore a dress," paint a picture with details about the color, style, and condition of the dress. Specific details help your readers imagine your characters more vividly.

4. **Give Your Characters Flaws and Quirks:** Perfect characters can be boring. Give your characters flaws, quirks, and contradictions to make them more interesting and relatable. Flaws can create drama and keep your readers hooked.

5. **Let Your Characters Interact:** Characters shine when they interact with others. Think about how your characters' relationships shape who they are. Dialogue and conflicts between characters can reveal a lot about their personalities.

6. **Think about Character Growth:** Consider how your characters change and grow throughout your story. A great character should have a journey or arc that shows development or transformation by the end of the story.

In conclusion, characters are key to making your story come alive. By creating characters with depth, flaws, specific details, and relationships, you can make your short stories really pop. Remember to show, not tell, and let your characters drive the story forward with their actions and decisions. Have fun writing your next masterpiece!

Unleash Your Creativity: Crafting Compelling Characters in Your Comic!

Hey, young comic creators! Today, we're diving into the exciting world of character creation for your comics. Characters are the superheroes, villains, and sidekicks who bring your comic to life, so let's learn how to make them truly compelling and unforgettable.

1. **Develop Unique Powers or Abilities:** Think about what makes each of your characters special. Do they have superpowers, unique abilities, or special skills? Consider how these powers can shape their personality and role in your comic's story.

2. **Design Memorable Visuals:** Visuals are key in comics! Design your characters with distinctive features, costumes, and expressions that make them stand out on the page. Think about colors, shapes, and symbols that represent your characters' personalities.

3. **Create Backstories:** Give your characters depth by creating backstories that explain their origins, motivations, and personal struggles. Backstories can add layers to your characters and make them more relatable to readers.

4. **Establish Strong Personalities:** Think about your character's personality traits: Are they brave, funny, cunning, or shy? Show these traits through their actions, dialogue, and interactions with other characters in your comic.

5. **Develop Relationships:** Characters shine when they interact with others. Explore how your characters' relationships with each other can add depth and drama to your comic. Friendships, rivalries, and alliances can all make your characters more dynamic and interesting.

6. **Create Character Arcs:** Just like in a story, characters in comics should experience growth and change over time. Consider giving your characters arcs that show development or transformation as the comic progresses. This can keep readers engaged and invested in your characters' journeys.

In conclusion, crafting compelling characters is essential to creating a captivating comic. By developing unique powers, memorable visuals, backstories, strong personalities, relationships, and character arcs, you can bring your characters to life in a way that will leave a lasting impact on your readers. So, grab your pens and let your imagination soar as you create your next comic masterpiece!

Level Up Your Game: Creating Compelling Characters for Video Games!

Hey, gamers and game developers-in-training! Today, we're going to explore the exciting world of character creation for video games. Characters are the heroes, villains, allies, and NPCs (non-playable characters) whom players connect with throughout their gaming experience. Let's learn how to craft characters who will truly captivate and engage players.

1. **Define Character Roles and Goals:** Start by defining the role of your characters in the game. Are they the main protagonist, a sidekick, a boss, or an NPC? What are their goals and motivations, and how do they fit into the game's storyline?

2. **Design Unique Visuals:** Visual design is crucial in video games. Create characters with distinctive appearances, outfits, and animations that make them visually appealing and easily recognizable. Consider their color palette, shapes, and overall aesthetic to ensure they stand out in the game world.

3. **Establish Backstories and Lore:** Give your characters depth by developing rich backstories, histories, and lore that explain their origins and shape their personalities. Consider how their past experiences influence their actions and decisions in the game.

4. **Create Engaging Personalities:** Characters in video games should have unique personalities that make them memorable and relatable to players. Consider traits like bravery, humor, intelligence, or cunning, and showcase these traits through their dialogue, interactions, and behavior in the game.

5. **Integrate Character Progression:** Just as in a story, characters in video games should experience growth and development as the game progresses. Think about how your characters evolve, gain new abilities, or face challenges that test their abilities and resolve.

6. **Foster Player-Character Connection:** Encourage players to connect with your characters emotionally by creating opportunities for meaningful interactions, dialogues, and choices that impact the characters' journeys and relationships within the game world.

In conclusion, creating compelling characters is essential to crafting an immersive and engaging gaming experience. By defining character roles, designing unique visuals, establishing backstories, creating engaging personalities, integrating character progression, and fostering player-character connections, you can create characters that players will remember long after they've put down the controller. So power up your creativity and start creating characters that will level up your game to new heights!

Tune In to Creating Compelling Characters for Your Fictional Podcast!

Hey, budding podcast creators! Today, we're diving into the world of character creation for your fictional podcast. Characters are the voices and personalities that will captivate your listeners and keep them coming back for more. Let's learn how to craft characters that will make your podcast truly unforgettable.

1. **Develop Unique Voices and Personalities:** Each character in your podcast should have a distinctive voice and personality that sets them apart. Consider their tone, speech patterns, quirks, and mannerisms to make them come alive through audio.

2. **Create Backstories and Motivations:** Give your characters depth by developing backstories, motivations, and personal histories that explain who they are and why they do what they do. Backstories can help listeners connect with your characters on a deeper level.

3. **Establish Relationships and Dynamics:** Characters in a podcast often interact with each other, so think about the relationships and dynamics between your characters. Whether they're friends, enemies, allies, or rivals, their interactions can add drama and depth to your storytelling.

4. **Introduce Intriguing Character Arcs:** Consider how your characters evolve and change over the course of your podcast. Give them arcs that show growth, transformation, or challenges that shape their journeys throughout the episodes.

5. **Use Sound Design to Enhance Characters:** Sound effects, music, and ambient noise can enhance your characters and bring them to life in your podcast. Consider how audio cues can reflect your characters' emotions, environments, and actions.

6. **Engage Listeners with Compelling Dialogue:** Dialogue is key in a podcast. Write engaging, authentic dialogue that reveals your characters' personalities, conflicts, and motivations. Use conversations to drive the plot forward and keep listeners hooked.

In conclusion, creating compelling characters is essential to crafting a captivating fictional podcast. By developing unique voices, backstories, relationships, character arcs, sound design, and engaging dialogue, you can create characters who will draw listeners into your world and keep them eagerly tuning in for each new episode. So grab your microphone, hit Record, and let your characters take centre stage in your podcast storytelling adventure!

Pembroke Publishers © 2025 *Students in the Driver's Seat* by Erin Quinn and Tara Vandertoorn ISBN 978-1-55138-373-6 

Lights, Camera, Action: Crafting Compelling Characters for Your Film Script!

Hey, future filmmakers! Today, we're stepping into the world of character development for your film script. Characters are the heart and soul of any movie, so let's explore how to create characters that will captivate audiences and bring your story to life on the big screen.

1. **Establish Clear Goals and Motivations:** Start by defining your characters' goals, desires, and motivations within the context of your film's storyline. What do they want? What drives them to take action? Understanding these key elements will help shape your characters' journeys throughout the script.

2. **Create Multidimensional Characters:** Avoid one-dimensional characters by giving them depth and complexity. Consider the strengths, weaknesses, fears, and internal conflicts that make them relatable and interesting to viewers. Complex characters are more engaging and memorable.

3. **Show, Don't Tell:** Instead of telling the audience about your characters, show them through their actions, dialogue, and interactions with other characters. Let the audience uncover your characters' traits, emotions, and motivations through visual storytelling.

4. **Develop Character Relationships:** Characters come alive when they interact with others. Explore the dynamics between your characters and how their relationships evolve throughout the film. Friendships, romances, rivalries, and conflicts can add layers to your characters and drive the plot forward.

5. **Introduce Character Arcs:** Every compelling character should undergo growth or change over the course of the film. Create character arcs that show development, transformation, or resolution for your characters by the end of the story. Audiences love to see characters evolve.

6. **Use Dialogue to Reveal Character:** Dialogue is a powerful tool for revealing your characters' personalities, conflicts, and emotions. Write authentic, engaging dialogue that reflects your characters' unique voices and drives the narrative forward.

In conclusion, crafting compelling characters is essential to creating a successful film script. By establishing clear goals, creating multidimensional characters, showing rather than telling, developing relationships, introducing character arcs, and using dialogue effectively, you can bring your characters to life on screen and immerse audiences in your storytelling world. So grab your script, bring your characters to life, and get ready to see them shine on the silver screen!

Student-Designed Projects

What Is It?

Inquiry-based learning is a topic that could fill a whole other book (and has!). In student-designed projects, a model of inquiry-based learning, however, the student is using their own interests, ideas, preferences, and strengths to self-design a project to demonstrate selected learning outcomes or standards. The teacher creates workflows, planning tools, and scaffolds to support the student in designing a project to demonstrate mastery of the outcome. The student must then learn the content and skills in order to demonstrate the outcomes.

Why Do It? Peeling Back the Pedagogy

This model of task design truly puts the student in the driver's seat. Though the outcome(s) or standard(s) are determined by the teacher, the student has free rein to design a project of their choice. This model of task design is one of the most student-centric models in this book as there are very few limits placed on what the students do or create to demonstrate their learning.

We suggest that some familiarity or comfort with student voice and choice is necessary for both teacher and students when offering this option to your students. If students are not practiced in making choices for themselves, unlimited choice can be scary. If the teacher is comfortable with this level of open-endedness but the students don't have the historical practice in working independently in the way self-designed projects demand, the teacher can support the students in scaffolded ways through a student-designed project.

Student-designed projects can come at the end of a unit and be a final summative task in which students can demonstrate the skills and content they have learned. They can also be structured as a unit themselves, with the opportunities to learn skills and content built into the design of the project.

How to Do It

Student-designed projects require very deliberate planning to support the students in designing projects that fully demonstrate their understanding of the outcome(s) you need them to show. Our favorite way to design projects such as these is using chart paper and sticky notes that can be moved around. We've outlined our process below.

1. Determine the outcome or cluster of outcomes you want students to demonstrate their understanding of. Write this at the top of your chart paper. If you have several outcomes, can you synthesize them into one succinct goal that can become your student prompt? For example, if you want students to demonstrate their understanding of different rhetorical devices, your prompt could become "Create a project that persuades someone to do something, think something, or act in a certain way. Use logos, pathos, and ethos effectively in your project."

2. Working backwards, what skills, knowledge, and understanding do your students need to know in order to show mastery of the outcome(s)? Write these on sticky notes.

3. What do you imagine your students could do to demonstrate the outcome(s)? Write down as many possibilities as you can think of on sticky notes. Note that you will not be giving these ideas to students necessarily, but brainstorming different ways students could respond

to your prompt helps to confirm whether your prompt is open-ended enough to allow for many different responses.

4. Design a tool such as a planning sheet or a graphic organizer your students can use to plan their projects. Make sure your prompt is clearly communicated on this planning sheet. Consider supporting your students in chunking their projects by breaking down the time they have to work on their projects. This will support your students in setting realistic goals for themselves in terms of the amount of time they have to complete the project and ensuring the complexity of the work reflects their timelines.

5. Depending on whether your student-designed project comes at the end of a unit or is replacing the unit itself, consider how you will support your students in incorporating the necessary knowledge and skills:

    a. If the project comes at the end of a unit, list the skills and knowledge the students have developed through the unit as resources the students can draw from to demonstrate their knowledge. In the above example of rhetorical devices, reminding students of the different speeches, advertisements, and pieces of writing where they saw logos, pathos, and ethos demonstrated will serve as a de facto "cheat sheet" for them to review the skills they are being asked to demonstrate in their project.

    b. If the project is taking the place of a unit, you will need to incorporate minilessons or resources to support the students in developing the skills required. Using our example, you could add a minilesson each day on logos, pathos, and ethos using carefully selected advertisements or micro mentor texts as examples. The minilessons could end with a call to action, inviting your students to incorporate this strategy into their project design. These minilessons could be delivered live to the class or be recorded and accessed on-demand from a learning management system like Google Classroom.

6. Design an assessment tool that is open enough to allow for many different interpretations of the outcome(s). The beauty of this approach to task design is that it is laser-focused on the outcome or standard. Success should be measured by how well students demonstrate the outcome.

7. Once the project is designed, get out of the way! Be prepared to spend a good chunk of time brainstorming ideas with your students to create a bank of ideas they can draw from. Watch your students blossom as they tap into their own interests and the ways of working that they enjoy to show you what they know.

The Tool in Practice

In my grade-nine English language arts curriculum, one of the big ideas that was present in many different outcomes was the idea of theme. This was something we had been building our understanding of throughout the year, and my students were ready not just to identify it in texts that other people had created but to create their own. I decided to facilitate a student-designed project in which they could develop a theme through a text they created.

I started by brainstorming different ways the students might do this, and we came up with a wide variety of texts that could contain theme: short stories, poems, songs, graphic novels, films, collections of artwork or photos, picture books, advertisements, and many more. Theme itself was so wide open, and I knew I would have to support each of my students in developing a theme they truly believed in and had something to say about: good vs. evil, love, identity, power and control, friendship, authenticity, freedom, mortality, justice, living a meaningful life, etc.! Knowing that identifying a theme my students had something to say something about needed to be the first step, I designed a graphic organizer with some examples of themes and a process to follow to narrow one of these broad themes down to something more specific. In the hands of my students, the ideas they settled on were as diverse as my students. Predictably, as I was working with teenagers, many of them settled on power, control, or justice as their themes, but their interpretations of these themes ran the gamut from overbearing helicopter parents to getting revenge on a bully to someone navigating a popular clique in school.

Next, I designed a planning sheet where each student could start with their theme and then select a mode and sketch out a storyline to reveal this theme. On the planning sheet, I included a blank calendar with our deadline marked, so students could work out how to chunk their projects into smaller parts. Before I gave this to my students, I spent a long time talking about different modes we had looked at previously in our English class as well as other modes from their own lives — TikTok videos, Instagram reels, and webcomics were all types of storytelling my students were very familiar with and could select for this project. I had my students sit in groups with a stack of sticky notes and a marker and brainstorm as many different storytelling modes as they could think of. We stuck them all up on a wall in our classroom, and when I handed out the graphic organizers, students used this wall to choose a mode that felt exciting to them. Once they had chosen their modes, they spent some time taking their themes and breaking them down into a story they would tell. Then, they worked out the steps they would need to take to accomplish their end goal and placed these steps on their calendar breakdown. On the whiteboard, I had a sign-up list for students to conference with me when their planning sheets were done. I called students over to my conference space in the classroom to go over their plans, offer feedback, and sign the spot at the bottom of their planning sheets to indicate they were ready to get going.

Over the next couple of weeks, my students worked hard on their projects. What was most exciting to me, when I observed my class during their work periods, was the variety of things going on in the room. As I scanned the classroom, overhead lights off and lo-fi music playing on the classroom screen, I saw three girls sitting in comfy chairs in the corner with laptops open, typing away at stories they were writing. I looked over to the long table at the back where a student was using the classroom bin of markers to color his graphic novel. I peeked into the hallway where a student was using one of the school's video cameras to shoot a scene for her short film. And I scanned back over the desks and saw a student using an online animation program to create an animated video, another with Garage Band open, remixing his original song, and another with magazines he had brought from home, cutting out different images to create a shadow box diorama. Without fail, there was total engagement as my students were fully invested in the projects they designed.

After they put the finishing touches on their work, I had a final step planned: a reflective written assignment where I would ask them to identify the theme they selected and discuss how this theme came through in their work.

Walk and Talk

What Is It?

When working collaboratively, sometimes we get stuck. We have found that a great way for the two of us to get the ideas moving again is to have a walking meeting, but we hadn't really connected this practice to our teaching until we were trying to figure out how to get our classes outside and on the land more regularly. The walk-and-talk protocol was born.

Use this tool when you have a few questions that you want students to think about, discuss, and respond to. Students can also generate the questions. Ask your question and then go for a walk, preferably outside. While students are walking they can be talking about the question or not, but when you stop and circle up, everyone will share their answer.

Why Do It? Peeling Back the Pedagogy

Walking and talking is a great way to get ideas moving. The physical activity and change of scenery help to reset the brain and stimulate positive endorphins. It is important that you ask your question before you begin walking as it gives processing time to students so that they can be prepared to share when you pause. The sharing occurs in a circle so that everyone can be seen and heard.

How To Do It

1. Identify the topic to be discussed and come up with a few questions. Head outside to your starting point and form a circle.
2. Introduce students to the protocol, or remind them about it and ask the first question. Students are encouraged to think and talk about their answers while walking. This protocol is grounded in the quote from Mae Jemison: "You have the right to be involved. You have something important to contribute, and you have to take the risk to contribute it."
   a. Everyone shares. You may "pass" but that means that I will return to you at the end. If you genuinely have no response then share your challenge with responding.
   b. No side conversations. Listen to understand.
   c. You don't have to talk about the question while walking but you do have to be prepared to thoughtfully respond when we stop.
3. Walk for a few minutes.
4. Stop and form a circle. Everyone shares their responses, including the teacher. Ask the next question.
5. Repeat.

The Tool in Practice

In a grade-nine social studies class, we had been learning about democracy and the role of a free press. As we gathered in a circle outside, I had the students quickly restate the protocol for a "Walk and Talk."

"It's a little cooler today, so let's get walking so we can warm up. Who can remind us all of our 'Walk and Talk' protocols? Khalid?"

"There's no point in passing because you just have to share at the end anyway," Khalid responded.

"And why is that?"

"Because everyone's contribution matters," he replied, only slightly rolling his fourteen-year-old eyes.

"Yes! You have something important to contribute but you have to take the risk to contribute it," I reminded the class. "Anything else?"

"Listen up," Eden called out.

"Yes. And on that note, listen up for our first question. Who do you consider to be 'the press?' Let's walk and talk."

We began the familiar path around the back of the school toward the end of the block. I fell in with a group of students debating whether a random person on TikTok sharing a video from a protest could be considered "the press." After a couple of minutes, we stopped and made a circle.

"Does anyone want to share first?" No hands went up. "Okay. We will start to my left but I'll go first so the first couple of people have these minutes while I'm talking to prepare themselves to share. I think that the idea of the press is becoming increasingly hard to define when everyone has a camera and a connection to a global audience but to me, a clear lack of bias is an important criterion. Chase, what do you think?"

We continued around the circle, and a few students did pass in the beginning but we came back around to them, and everyone had the chance to share.

"Next question: Do you think the press should have the right to totally free speech? Why or why not? Let's walk and talk."

This time I sped up and walked with a group in which a student had a clear, thoughtful response to the first question and I asked her if she could go first in the next circle. She agreed and she and her friends began discussing freedom of the press. When we circled up, Teigan volunteered to start off the sharing.

Once everyone had responded, I said, "Okay, last question for today. What do you look for in good reporting?" As students discussed the qualities of good reporting, there was laughter as some students shared examples of bad reporting.

We stopped one more time and our route eventually led us back to school. When we returned to class, I introduced our next assignment: Students would choose a type of media and create content on an issue of their choice.

PART 4

Assessment

One of the most profound discoveries we have made in our teaching practice is the understanding that assessment *is* teaching. When we make this shift, we open up possibilities. Rather than thinking that assessment is something that happens at the end of learning, assessment becomes part of the fabric of your classroom. Engaging in assessment with the students during the course of your class is transformative to your practice. We do not take grading home because the work is assessed with the student at school during class. This emphasizes the idea that assessment is not a separate activity or final measure of student performance, but an integral part of the teaching and learning process. Assessment is a tool for guiding instruction, providing feedback, and shaping the learning experience.

Assessment as teaching is also a formative practice in avoiding teacher burnout. If you're assessing in class you can avoid excessive work outside of the school day, which helps maintain a healthy relationship between instruction, assessment, and personal time.

We are going to talk about a hard reality here. Most of us are not using formative assessment to inform teaching. When students don't do well or haven't mastered a concept we either blame the learner, their behavior, or their circumstances. "Of course Ethan hasn't mastered fractions; he has missed 30% of classes," or, "I'm not surprised Kate didn't do well on her descriptive paragraph, she has a writing learning disability," or, "Jason is going to struggle this year given the trauma he has experienced," or, "I know some of these kids aren't going to do well on the test, but I don't have time to go back and reteach this material. The curriculum is too dense." Yes. These things all impact student performance. And, we have to be willing to put our egos aside as educators and allow for the opportunity assessment provides. How can we reteach a concept? How do we revisit a topic? How can we truly use assessment to inform teaching?

In a classroom oriented towards student voice and choice, much of the assessment process is oriented towards growth. Feedback moves learning forward and reveals next steps. Cycles of assessment are built into the design of the task and are full of checkpoints to monitor understanding and growth. In this model, not too much time passes before the teacher is able to provide the student with feedback. We are never looking at a final product as our first glance.

The timing of assessment is incredibly important for this very reason. We need opportunities to give feedback with enough time for it to be actioned. Feedback must inform the students' next steps. We must time the feedback so that the student sees the value in using the feedback immediately. Otherwise, it will be forgotten and will not move learning forward. Providing frequent opportunities for feedback helps you track student progress, identify learning gaps, and guide future teaching while there's still time to action the feedback — for both student and teacher.

Ideally, the student will have multiple opportunities to practice a skill and use the feedback to improve. More practice with a skill and more chances to incorporate the feedback mean that there's more likelihood the feedback will impact student learning. One example from our own classrooms is our approach to teaching annotation as a skill for doing a close reading of texts in our English language arts classroom. This is a skill we come back to again and again and constantly give feedback on. An approach we use often with this skill is the sticky note feedback protocol you'll see later in this chapter. When reading a novel, our students are writing their observations, thoughts, and questions in their notebooks as they read. As students are reading, we're circulating among them to peek over their shoulders at their annotations. We will then give a quick piece of feedback, such as, "Try to focus on making predictions in the next section," which we also jot down on a sticky note for the student so they can remember the feedback that was given. As students continue reading, they have an immediate opportunity to incorporate this feedback.

This is a good moment to note that self-reflection alone is not summative assessment. In fact, as a stand-alone practice it is often not even a very good formative assessment. Each of us is doing the best we can. Remembering this when it comes to students' self-assessment is essential. Despite your best laid rubrics and clearly explained instructions students sometimes do not do what you expect. Self-reflection often assumes intentionality in what has not been done well. We have found that when students who aren't meeting a standard of excellence talk about their work they know that it isn't excellent but they're often either resigned to it or ashamed about it. It is essential to shift the assessment conversation away from grades towards growth. There is something to celebrate in every student's work. We love to begin our assessment conversations by asking the student, "What are you most proud of in your work?".

While students can often identify what they need to improve, especially in conversation, if they knew how to improve most would have done it already. This is where your feedback becomes essential and where partnering with students in the assessment process matters. And asking students, "What do you need to know or learn to improve this?" can help you use assessment to actually improve teaching.

This shift in approaching assessment as part of the learning process has massive implications for you and your practice as a teacher. Marking can no longer take place at 9:00 p.m, when you're alone on your couch. Assessment must take place in the company of the students you teach. An added bonus to this means you're no longer taking home your "bag of good intentions," as Tara calls it. So, then, assessment has to take place *during* class time.

There are equally massive implications with this for your classroom management. You must be able to dedicate yourself to one-on-one conversations with students, and therefore, the rest of your students must be able to manage themselves and be independent in their learning while you do that. Of course, much of the solution to this lies in your task design, giving students work they are interested in, care about, and are able to accomplish independently. Designing tasks with engagement in mind can solve many of these problems because when students are doing work they care about, they're more likely to become absorbed in it. Good task design, however, is not enough.

Be prepared to find some holes in your classroom management. Both of us pride ourselves on having strong classroom management, but when we shifted to an assessment approach where conferencing with students was our major mode of assessment, there were days (and weeks!) when we were at our wits' end trying to put out fires and stop some students from disrupting others. So what did we do? We took a good look at the norms in our classrooms and involved our students to create, establish, and practice norms that emphasized productivity and focus. We also sharpened the procedures in our spaces, making sure our rooms flowed smoothly without our involvement. (We shared some of these procedures in the Introduction and Building a Toolkit section.) We also spent a good deal of energy and time working towards creating a strong classroom culture and setting the tone in the space. As mentioned, creating a culture where students respect and trust each other is key here. In addition to this, neither of us underestimates the role that the design of the classroom space plays in setting a good tone. Experiment with shutting off the fluorescent lights and using lamps or natural light instead. Allow students to use headphones to plug into computers. Bring in plants and greenery and remove visual clutter. Ensure the design of your space allows students to breathe and slow down.

When beginning this work, you'll need to give yourself and your students grace. You need to consider the historical experience of the students you are working with as you embark on more student voice and choice in assessment. When you are working with a group of students who are less experienced in making decisions and having input in assessment, there will be growing pains. Students such as these must be taught the executive functioning skills necessary to be able to make these choices. You may consider starting small, and beginning with informal types of assessment is a way you can begin to build up your students' stamina in these skills. When you shift from a compliance model towards one oriented towards engagement, the initial lack of forced compliance can feel chaotic. Students do not have the skills to make decisions because they have never been asked to do so before in a meaningful way. Know this, take a deep breath, and move forward. You will be teaching your students these skills as you trust them to become involved in making decisions in their own learning.

Ongoing and regular communication with home is also a key aspect of good assessment practice. Students need to clearly understand why they're doing the work and so do families. In recent conversation, there has been a lot of public energy wasted around the idea that teachers are teaching anything other than the mandated curriculum. Clearly connecting students' work to the learner outcomes mitigates these concerns. This chapter shares some ideas about how to celebrate student learning, but don't forget to include the why and how in those celebrations. Good assessment should never be a surprise and so allowing families to see why their child is doing the work and how they are doing compared to grade level expectations is an essential part of celebrating student success.

Two of the hallmarks of good assessment are recency and frequency. Integrating assessment into your teaching allows you to ensure that your results are evidence of current best practice. There has been considerable discussion recently about building equitable assessment practices, as in Joe Feldman's book *Grading for Equity* (2018). Involving students and their families in their assessment is one way we can bring equity to assessment practices.

Celebration of Learning

What Is It?

A celebration of learning is any event that showcases student work for an audience beyond the classroom. Students, teachers, and sometimes parents come together to showcase and celebrate the learning that students have done over a period of time, like a unit, semester, or entire year.

Why Do It? Peeling Back the Pedagogy

The pedagogy behind a celebration of learning is rooted in several key educational principles that promote active learning, student engagement, and reflection. Students are invited in as active participants in their learning, not just in creating the work but also in communicating their learning. This aligns with constructivist pedagogy (Ültanir, 2012) where students build their understanding through experience and reflection. By selecting and showcasing their work, students take ownership of their learning journey, which is crucial in student-centred learning as it increases motivation and engagement.

This type of assessment also encourages students to reflect on their progress and learning outcomes, helping to shift the focus to learning as a process. When students are selecting the work to showcase, they are identifying their strengths and areas for improvement. Incorporating the opportunity to receive feedback from teachers and peers also supports assessment as a guide to support learning, not just a grade.

These experiences provide positive reinforcement by recognizing students' hard work and achievements, supporting a growth mindset where challenges are viewed as opportunities rather than obstacles. When students receive positive feedback from the larger community it builds confidence and supports continued engagement in learning. When families are able to share in what their child is learning they are better able to engage with that learning at home, further driving the child's engagement at school. We all like to feel that people are interested in what we do.

How to Do It

Set Clear Objectives.

- What is the purpose of the celebration of learning? Is it to highlight a specific project, demonstrate mastery of skills, or reflect on growth over a period of time? Share the objective with your students to support them in self-selecting what to share.
- Aligning your celebration with specific learning outcomes or curriculum aspects will help to focus the event.

Choose a Format. Possibilities could include some or all of the following:

- Individual or group presentations: Will students present individually, in small groups, or as a class?
- Exhibition or showcase: Work is set up so visitors can walk around, interact, and ask questions.
- Performance: You can include plays, music, dance, or speeches that reflect what students have learned.
- Digital Presentations: Students can share slideshows, videos, or virtual galleries.

Prepare Students.

- Select work to showcase: Offer clear criteria for selection so that students can choose the work they are most proud of that best represents their learning. It is often beneficial if students know that they will be sharing work ahead of time so that they can keep this consideration in mind throughout the learning.
- Practice and Prepare: Students should participate in the set-up of the event so that they feel ownership. If they are speaking, allow time for practice.
- Reflect on Learning: This is a great opportunity to include student reflections on the learning journey. This could be in writing, as part of the presentation, or, a favourite of ours, as a pre-recorded statement connected to a scannable QR code that participants can listen to or view during the event.

Engage Your Community.

- Invite families and community members with enough notice that they can plan around the event. Including a simple digital RSVP can help you plan for numbers and connecting to other school events can increase attendance (for example, before a PTA meeting or a home sporting game).
- Collaborating with colleagues can also increase family attendance.
- Consider how you are inviting families. This is another opportunity to incorporate student voice and increase participation. Perhaps you have a few students who would like to design a digital invitation or create a program for the event?

Facilitate the Event.

- How will you welcome your guests?
- How will they flow through the event and the space(s)?
- What are the opportunities for interaction with you and with students?

Make Time for Reflection upon Completion.

- Gathering feedback from students, teachers, and attendees will help you understand what worked well and what could be improved for future events. This is a great opportunity to model a growth mindset and feedforward learning with your students.

The Tool in Practice

In the final month of grade six, we engaged our students in a variety of cross-curricular learning projects that asked them to apply and connect their learning from throughout the year. These projects took the place of a final exam, and we emphasized that each one should reflect the best work they were capable of producing. We called this culminating experience the "Museum of Grade Six Learning." Students had a lot of choice in both topic and format, but they knew that all their work would be shared. The projects invited them to reflect on who they were at the start of the year, who they had become, and who they hoped to be as they moved into grade seven.

We invited all of our families to a two-hour, open house–style event. Students set up their projects gallery-style so that, as families arrived, they could engage with work that showcased each student's growth and identity. The event was multimodal, featuring visuals, writing, audio, and video.

It proved to be a meaningful culmination of the year's learning. Parents shared that they appreciated not only seeing their child's work but also hearing their reflections on identity. At this age, students are often reluctant to open up at home, and families told us they had learned new things about their children—not just as learners but as people. Many said the event sparked deep and memorable conversations. We also heard that families enjoyed getting a glimpse into the lives and work of their child's peers.

Conferencing

What Is It?

Conferencing is probably the oldest form of assessment there is. There truly is no better or simpler way of finding out what a student knows and can do than having a conversation with them. Conferencing as a method of assessment is something that has long been a part of the writing workshop model but translates well to other subjects and content areas as well.

When the teacher meets with the student one-on-one, they look at the student's work together, discussing what the student is proud of, areas for growth, and sometimes determining a grade together. Conferencing can also be used at interim points in a project to check in on a student's progress and give feedback for next steps. Conferencing can be formal, where a schedule is set to meet with each student, or informal, where the teacher checks in with students as they are working.

Why Do It? Peeling Back the Pedagogy

Conferencing emphasizes student voice because it gives students an opportunity to drive the assessment conversation. It positions the assessment process toward generosity, encouraging both the student and the teacher to focus on the strengths of the work. It also encourages accountability. When a student has to discuss their work with their teacher, rather than just handing it in and hoping for the best, they're much more likely to put effort into making the work the best they can.

One of the most important reasons for conferencing is relationship building. We encourage the teacher to deliberately take a minute before looking at the work to chat with the student, ask how they are doing or what their plans for the weekend are. These few moments of genuine connection go far in developing caring relationships in the classroom. In a classroom full of dynamic personalities, it is easy to get to know some students more than others. Sometimes relationships with more introverted students are more difficult to forge, which is why conferencing is so helpful. It schedules teachers to talk to every student, not just the more outgoing ones who are easy to form relationships with. Building relationships is absolutely key to prioritizing voice and choice in the classroom. A safe, caring environment encourages students to feel comfortable taking risks, both academically and socially.

When conferencing with students, it is important to always give the student the final say in how they use the feedback they receive in the conference. When the feedback is connected to the criteria or learning outcomes of the task, and students decide not to incorporate the feedback given, they also accept the consequences of this associated with grading. When the feedback is more stylistic, we position the student as the creator of this text and empower them to make the decisions associated with this role.

How to Do It

There are many different ways to set up conferencing. Here are a few of our favorites.

Informal Conferencing

One way to do informal conferencing is to create a chart or documentation sheet for the class and carry it around on a clipboard as you circulate while students work. You can use this tracking sheet to document student progress as they work towards their goals. This is most effective if you have something specific you are looking for while students work. As you circulate and give feedback to students, checking for understanding, you can record on your documentation sheet what the student has demonstrated. We like to use a Check, Check Plus, or Minus to record whether the student is demonstrating the skill, demonstrating the skill with mastery, or not yet demonstrating the skill.

Another way to do informal conferencing is regular check-ins with students over the course of a project or throughout a year or term. This method of conferencing will be familiar to teachers who have done reading or writing workshops (see, for example, Atwell, 2007). Teachers meet regularly with students at points during the project, discussing their progress and next steps. This is an opportunity to reteach a skill that is not yet mastered. Documentation of student progress in this method often takes the form of a tracking sheet for each student. A teacher might have a binder with a divider for each student, recording what was discussed with each student during each conference.

One final way we love to use informal conferencing is at certain checkpoints in a project. This utilizes the protocol in the Building a Toolkit section called Checklists. For example, perhaps you have students working on a writing project in which they're researching a topic that interests them, organizing their ideas, and creating a piece of writing about their topic. In this method, students are given a set of instructions for the whole project, with each step broken down. At the end of each section of the project, an assessment checkpoint is built into the project sheet. When students reach that point in the project, they must check in with the teacher to ensure they are ready to move on to the next section. In our example, the student might have finished their research notes and think they're ready to move into their planning phase. The student will then check in with the teacher, and a quick conference will happen. The teacher will look at the student's research notes, determine if the criteria for this part of the project have been met, and give the student the go-ahead to move on to their planning. One thing we like to do on our project sheets is have a spot for the teacher's initials or signature at the end of each section, and a space to record feedback. The teacher's signature is the student's "ticket" to move on to the next phase of the project.

Formal Conferencing

1. Establish a conference schedule. To do this, determine how much time you want to give to each conference. This will depend on the depth and scope of the work. If it is a quick check-in to discuss next steps, two minutes can be enough. If you need time to really look at the work and discuss it, five to ten minutes per student may be needed.
2. Make a plan for what the other students will be doing while you conference. The questions we most often get when we discuss

conferencing is, "What is the rest of the class doing? How do I prevent the class from devolving into chaos while I talk to one student?" When using conferencing during writing or reading, the answer is quite simple: the students are reading or writing while you are conferencing. If used at the end of a formal assignment, like an essay or project, the answer to this question can be more complicated. Students should be able to work on whatever task they are doing while you are conferencing with students independently so they do not interrupt you. The task also needs to be within an appropriate level of challenge for all students. Students who are stuck or frustrated with a task are more likely to get distracted or off task and disrupt others' learning. Some teachers set aside time at a designated point during a work period for conferencing, such as during a bellwork-type activity where all students are working independently.

3. Call students over to a conferencing area or go to them at their desks. Both methods have their benefits. Conferencing at the teacher's desk or at a designated conferencing space creates some privacy for the student where they are away from their peers. It also gives the teacher access to a computer, often, which can be helpful for recording notes or assessment data from the conference in an online gradebook if desired. Conferencing at the student's desk brings the teacher into the student's space, which can set the student at ease and break down divides.

4. As discussed, we like to begin the conversation by asking the student a question unrelated to the work. Then we dig into it together. We like to take a moment to first look at the work and ask the student to explain what they did. "Tell me what you did here," is a very obvious but very powerful question that gets the student to explain what stood out to them about the process. The next question we like to ask is, "What are you most proud of?" This question focuses the conversation towards the student's strengths. Usually, the student is quite self-aware of their own strengths, and nine times out of ten, what the student identifies as a strength in the work is an area we identify as a strength also.

5. The next step of the conference is to discuss feedback for next steps. It's best if this piece of feedback is something the student can work on immediately in the next piece of work they are doing. Show the student where in their work the next step would be situated.

6. Have a grading conversation, if desired. If the conference is at the end of an assignment or project, looking at a rubric or set of criteria together with the student can be the last step of the conference. We often like to ask the student which grade they have demonstrated using the assessment criteria to ground this conversation. If students have never been asked this question before, they might respond with an "I don't know." If this happens, read through the assessment criteria together.

7. If you use an online gradebook, an additional step we like to take at this moment in the conference is to record the grade and a comment with the student present. We like to compose the comment with the student present so they are aware of and a part of what goes into their gradebook. Taking the extra minute to create a comment about what the student demonstrated in the task can make parent communication a lot easier and can be a time saver when it comes to complete report cards and you need to remember what the student did.

The Tool in Practice

Independent reading was a practice that my students engaged in during the first fifteen minutes of our grade-nine English language arts class all semester long. My students entered the room, grabbed their self-selected reading books and their reading notebooks, and found a comfortable place to read. After everyone had entered the class, found their spot, and settled into their reading, I began conferencing. Because I didn't want to distract the students by calling them over, I opted to go to them for our reading conferences.

I wheeled my stool over to Claire, who was sitting in a beanbag chair by the window, *Firekeeper's Daughter* by Angeline Boulley in her lap. Her reading notebook was on the floor beside her, with her pencil marking her page.

"How are you today, Claire?" I asked in a whisper.

"Pretty good."

"Did you do anything fun this weekend?" I asked.

"Nothing much. I had a hockey game on Saturday. Then we went to my grandma's for supper yesterday."

"That sounds nice. Sometimes it's nice to have kind of low-key weekends. So, how's the book?"

"Oh my gosh, so good. I'm just at the part when Daunis is agreeing to go undercover. I would be so scared if I was her."

"May I?" I gestured at her reader's notebook, opening to the page her pencil was marking. I read her notes. I saw predictions, and notes tracking the major plot points and characterization. I also saw she was making connections, noting other books and TV shows the book reminded her of.

"What are you most proud of in your reader's notebook this time?" I asked.

"I think I'm doing a good job making sure I'm going beyond just the literal parts of the book. I'm not just summarizing, I'm making connections and predictions."

"I agree. This part right here where you've made connections between the character of Jamie in *Firekeeper's Daughter* and Jimmy in the TV show *Shameless* is really interesting. That's not a connection that would have occurred to me!"

"Oh, thanks. I binged that show last summer hard," she laughed.

"A nice next step for you would be to start noting some of the author's moves you notice. For example, what do you notice about how Boulley is creating suspense?"

"Ah, okay. So, like, when I feel nervous about what's going to happen next, I should stop and notice what the author's doing to make me feel that way?"

"Exactly. Give it a try over the next little bit and we'll check in again in a couple of weeks."

I jotted down a few notes on the documentation sheet in the binder I had on my lap: *Claire is making strong connections between characters in her book and other texts. Next step: Noticing author's craft.*

I wheeled my stool over to the next student.

Self-Reflection Tools

What Is It?

Self-reflection refers to the process by which students critically evaluate their own learning experiences, assignments, and thought processes. It involves students considering what they have learned, how they have learned it, and how they can apply that learning going forward. It encourages them to be active participants in their learning journeys, which can lead to deeper understanding and personal growth.

Why Do it? Peeling Back the Pedagogy

Supporting students with self-reflection leads to deeper understanding and retention of material as they consider what they have learned and what they still need to understand. As they reflect, they are encouraged to think critically about the material they are learning, moving beyond surface-level memorization to a deeper understanding of concepts. Reflection supports students in making connections which lead to more meaningful learning. Through self-reflection students become empowered to take control of their own learning and are able to make informed decisions about next steps. The self-awareness that is built through the reflection process helps students monitor and regulate their thinking. This leads to greater motivation and engagement, fosters critical thinking and problem-solving, and helps develop more autonomy.

Self-reflection also supports differentiation as both students and teachers become more aware of individual student needs, strengths, and challenges. Teachers can offer more personalized support and resources to address specific learning needs. And self-reflection can provide insights to support teachers in refining instructional strategies to better meet students' needs. As students reflect on their strengths and their challenges and setbacks, they learn to view mistakes as learning opportunities. This further develops their ability to persevere when faced with the next challenge. Overall, self-reflection contributes to deeper learning, better engagement, and more effective and responsive teaching.

How to Do It

There are several different types of self-reflection that can occur in a classroom.

- Learning Process Evaluation: Students reflect on how they approached their assignment considering what strategies were used and if they were effective. This can include the method of learning, time management, and problem-solving strategies used.
- Understanding and Mastery: Students gauge their level of understanding and identify gaps in their knowledge, recognizing areas for continued study.
- Goal Setting: One of the most common results of reflection is when students set personal or academic goals based on their current progress.
- Feedback Interpretation: The process of reflecting on feedback from peers or teachers, considering how it applies to their work, and how they can use it to improve helps students become more receptive to constructive criticism.

The Tool in Practice

In my sixth-grade classroom, several students were completing a songwriting assignment—a project where they wrote their own original songs, focusing on the lyrics as a form of poetry. This was one of the options for the final project in our poetry unit, and Maya, in particular, had been looking forward to it all month. She was most engaged when we analyzed song lyrics, clearly connecting to the song as a poetic form. The task was to create verses that told a story, expressed an emotion, or painted a vivid picture, using poetic techniques like rhyme, meter, and imagery.

Students shared their final projects either through publication—posting a final draft for our class gallery walk—or through performance, sharing their work aloud with the class. After everyone had a chance to share, we gathered for a reflection session. We regularly used "glow" (something they felt they did well) and "grow" (something they wanted to improve) as our framework for reflection. Sometimes students did this in writing, sometimes in one-on-one or small-group conferences, and sometimes as a whole class. It was May, and we had built a strong classroom community, so students felt comfortable reflecting together as a group. When it was Maya's turn, she looked thoughtful as she began to speak.

"For my glow, I think I did a really good job with the imagery in my song," she said. "I worked hard to create pictures with my words, like when I described the autumn leaves falling and the wind whispering through the trees. I think that part of my song really helped to set the mood and make the listener feel like they were there."

I smiled, remembering how vividly Maya had described the changing seasons in her lyrics. Her words had a way of transporting the reader to the scene she was painting, and I knew from her previous work that she had a natural talent for creating strong, evocative images with her writing.

"For my grow," she continued, "I think I need to work on the structure of my verses. I noticed that some of my lines didn't flow as smoothly as I wanted, and the rhythm felt a bit off in some places. I want to get better at making sure my lines flow more."

I nodded, appreciating Maya's insight. She had not only identified her strength in using imagery but also recognized the importance of rhythm and structure in poetry. It was clear she understood how these elements worked together to create a cohesive and impactful piece of writing.

"That's a great observation, Maya," I said. "Your imagery is powerful, and it really brings your song to life. Working on the rhythm and structure is a great goal, and it will make your poetry even stronger."

As we continued around the room, I noticed that Maya's thoughtful self-reflection inspired her classmates to think more deeply about their own writing. Each student's "glow" and "grow" provided valuable insights into their creative process, and I was pleased to see them taking ownership of their development as writers.

Later that day, Maya approached me and asked if she could spend some extra time working on her poem. She was determined to refine the rhythm of her verses and make her song even more polished. Watching her dedication to improving her craft, I couldn't help but feel proud. This moment highlighted the importance of self-reflection as it helped students recognize their potential and motivated them to keep growing as writers and thinkers.

Sticky Note Feedback

What Is It?

Sticky note feedback is the process by which a teacher circulates throughout the room as students are working, checking in on students to see how they are progressing in their work. These check-ins can be initiated by the teacher or the student. Students might ask the teacher for help, reassurance, or guidance as they work. Other times, teachers might use sticky note feedback as a formative assessment tool.

When a teacher is circulating in the room to discuss next steps in learning with students, the teacher is armed with a pack of sticky notes, jotting down next steps as they talk. Then the teacher leaves each student with a sticky note so the student has a visible reminder of what they discussed. It is helpful to date the note or use different-colored notes for each visit. This can help the teacher keep track of which students they have already given feedback to and which students they still need to visit.

As mentioned, this protocol pairs well with the informal feedback strategy.

Why Do It? Peeling Back the Pedagogy

All teachers can relate to this scenario: You spend hours grading and leaving comments on a set of student projects and hand them back to your students only to find half of them in your recycling bin at the end of the day, comments unread. Feedback is one of the most powerful tools a teacher has to move student learning forward. But it is only powerful if the student hears it and then applies it.

Sticky note feedback works to solve both these problems. Rather than having the student read feedback after the assignment is over, feedback is offered in the moment, while the student is working. The feedback offered can be immediately applied. To capture the feedback and make sure it doesn't disappear into the ether just to be forgotten, a quick note is jotted down and given to the student to serve as a reminder of what was discussed.

This is a universal strategy that can support students in all learning scenarios but is particularly helpful when students are working on projects that involve voice and choice. This is because the feedback each student receives needs to be specific to their own work and applicable to their own unique next step in learning. This tool works especially well in our complex classrooms because the teacher can connect the feedback specifically to the challenge that is right for each learner.

In the beginning, this strategy can feel a bit time-consuming as you write a unique comment for every student. As you do it you will start to see commonalities in the feedback you're giving, and you may even develop a mental comment bank for the most common feedback you give. You will also notice patterns in your classroom. In this way, sticky note feedback can also become informal assessment that drives teaching, highlighting areas that you need to review for students.

How to Do It

1. Ensure all students are on task and working on their projects.
2. Once everyone has settled into their work, begin circulating to check in with students. Bring a pad of sticky notes and something to write with along with you. We like to get down on our students' level by pulling up a chair alongside their workspace. We want the feedback we're about to offer to be supportive and noncritical, and getting on their level is one way we can set the tone for this.
3. Look at what the student is working on. A question like, "How's it going?" or, "What are you working on now?" is a great way to get the conversation going. Once the student has given you context, take a look at the work. Think about what piece of feedback can support the student in getting to their next right step. Angela Stockman (2023) frames feedback as

either warm or cool, with warm feedback being something that you notice is a strength or something that stands out in the work, and cool feedback as being a next step or something to work on. The best feedback conversations involve both warm and cool feedback. At the end of your conversation, jot down the next steps on the sticky note and stick it on the student's desk or in their notebook.

4. Thank the student for sharing their work with you, and continue on to the next student.

The Tool in Practice

"Today we're going to continue working on our water experiments," I explained. "Your goal is to make sure you've got your hypothesis done. Since everyone is working on a different kind of project, my work today is to come around and check in with you to see how you're doing. Are there questions right now that everyone would benefit from hearing?"

"Can we sit where we want?" Sam asked, as I knew he would. He asked every day. The class laughed.

"What am I going to say?" I replied.

"As long as you're productive and working!" the class parroted back.

"As long as you're productive and working," I confirmed. "Okay, let's get started. Focused and productive are the norms of the day!"

A few students moved seats, opened up their laptops, and pulled open their projects. I scanned the room, looking for students who might need some support in getting started. I helped Janae set up a table in her document, and helped Keeyan find a reliable website about the effects of climate change on the oceans. Soon the clattering of computer keys filled the air. What I thought of as triage was done, and now we were ready to dig in.

I grabbed my favorite turquoise sticky notes and my pen and wheeled my stool over to Santiago, who was working on his laptop at one of the round tables at the back of the room.

"How's it going, Santi?" I asked.

"Okay. I've finished my introduction and I've started my hypothesis," he replied.

"Remind me what you're investigating again?"

"Microplastics in drinking water," he replied.

"Ah, yes. Can I take a look?" He tilted his computer screen so I could see. I read his introduction.

"Your introduction is very strong. This part here where you're discussing the products that people are using that have microplastics in them without them knowing it is really good. I think the effect is that your audience is going to be drawn into the topic, because so many people wear fleece without knowing it contributes to microplastics every time you wash it," I said, being deliberate in explaining the effect the choice he made in his writing would have.

I looked at what he had so far for his hypothesis. "So you've got your question here already, which is a great first step. Can different water filtration systems filter out microplastics from our drinking water? Remember that a strong hypothesis makes a statement about a relationship. What will your independent variable be? Different filtration techniques?"

He nodded. "Yeah, I'm going to try different kinds of filters and then look at the filtered samples under the microscope to see which method worked well."

"Okay, then you need to make a prediction about which method you think might work the best and then state it as a relationship. You can start by phrasing it as an if/then statement, and then wordsmith it from there." On a sticky note, I wrote, "Phrase hypothesis as a relationship. Start with If… then…"

I placed the sticky note on his science notebook sitting on his table.

"Thanks for sharing your work with me. Your experiment is off to a great start. Can't wait to see what you do next!" I enthused. "Do you have any more questions for me?" I asked.

"Nope, I'm good to go!" Santi replied.

I wheeled my stool away and pulled it up to the next student and started again.

Student-Led Parent-Teacher Interviews

What Is It?

Student-led parent-teacher conferences are a powerful tool for fostering engagement, self-awareness, and community in the classroom. In this model, students take the lead in sharing their learning with their families, using selected pieces of work to highlight their growth, achievements, and challenges. This approach shifts the focus from a one-sided conversation between parents and teachers to a collaborative dialogue where students take ownership of their learning journey.

Unlike traditional conferences, which often centre on a teacher's perspective, student-led conferences allow students to choose what to showcase and how to present it. They might explain a science experiment, share a piece of creative writing, or walk their family through a recent math project—whatever best reflects their progress and goals. Teachers act as facilitators, providing students with tools and frameworks to prepare, while families gain a unique window into their child's learning process. The result is an experience that not only celebrates student voice but also builds deeper connections between home and school.

Why Do It? Peeling Back the Pedagogy

Student-led parent-teacher conferences are a research-backed practice that enhances student engagement and accountability. By allowing students to present their progress and learning experiences, these conferences foster a sense of ownership and responsibility. This active participation encourages self-reflection and goal setting, which are crucial for personal and academic growth (Nauss, 2010).

Research indicates that student-led conferences strengthen the relationship between students and teachers, promoting collaboration and trust (Amos, 2022). This collaborative environment supports students in identifying strategies critical to their success. Additionally, involving students in the conference process provides greater insight into their needs, enabling parents and teachers to better understand how students learn and where support is needed. In this way, students become active participants in the assessment of their learning. In student-led conferences, "education stops being something done to them and begins being something that *they are leading*" (Berger, 2014).

Moreover, student-led conferences establish a feedback loop that enhances communication and dialogue among students, parents, and teachers. This process moves away from focusing solely on grades, emphasizing the learning journey and the development of leadership skills (Şişman and Bahadır, 2021).

Engaging students in this manner encourages them to take risks and invest in their learning, knowing they have their teacher's support.

Student-led conferences are an established educational practice that empowers students, fosters collaboration, and provides valuable insights into student learning, all of which contribute to student success.

How to Do It

The research of Little and Allan (1989) started a foundational three-step model for student-led conferencing: Prepare, implement, and evaluate. This process has continued to evolve and change and there are a wide variety of models available. The basic structure and key considerations are as follows.

Prepare.

Introduce the Process: Explain the purpose of student-led conferences to your students. Highlight how these conferences encourage ownership of learning, self-reflection, and communication. Share examples of what a successful conference might look like to build understanding and confidence.

Link Learning to the Curriculum: Guide students in selecting work that reflects their progress in relation to specific curricular outcomes. This could include assignments, projects, or assessments that demonstrate their achievements and areas for growth. Encourage students to identify where they have met or exceeded expectations and where they are still working toward mastery.

Teach Reflection: Provide students with tools to reflect on their learning, such as prompts tied to curricular goals. For instance, in math, they might explain how their problem-solving strategies have evolved, or in language arts, how their writing reflects key skills like sentence fluency or idea development. Reflection strengthens students' ability to articulate their learning journey.

Implement.

Student as Leader: During the conference, students take charge of sharing their selected work and explaining their learning progress. They should connect their achievements and challenges directly to the curriculum, using the language of the outcomes to show how their learning aligns with classroom goals.

Encourage Family Involvement: Parents or guardians should be invited to ask open-ended questions that deepen the conversation, such as, "What part of this project was most challenging?" or "What skills do you feel more confident in now?" This creates a supportive environment for meaningful dialogue. Teachers may provide families with a handout with some guiding questions to support this involvement.

Teacher as Facilitator: The teacher's role is to provide support as needed. Step in to clarify curricular outcomes, guide discussions, or add insights to help connect the student's reflections to their future learning.

Evaluate.

Create Actionable Next Steps: Collaboratively identify next steps that are directly tied to the curriculum. For example, a student might set a goal to improve in multiplying fractions or to integrate stronger transitions in their writing. Ensure these goals are tied to specific classroom learning targets.

Monitor and Adjust: Plan regular follow-ups to check on students' progress toward their goals. Use these opportunities to celebrate successes, reassess challenges, and refine plans as needed. This ongoing process keeps students motivated and accountable.

- Portfolio Showcases: Students curate a portfolio of their work to demonstrate learning in multiple subject areas. They present this portfolio during the conference, tying their reflections to curricular outcomes.
- Learning Stations: For younger students, stations highlighting key areas of learning (e.g., literacy, numeracy, science, social studies) can help organize the conversation. Students guide parents through each station, explaining their progress and goals.
- Goal-Focused Conferences: These conferences emphasize how students are progressing toward curricular goals. Students discuss specific outcomes, such as mastering multiplication or developing narrative writing skills, and how they plan to address areas for growth.

The Tool in Practice

I sat at the back of the classroom, watching as Tenzin adjusted the pages in his portfolio. His mom, Mrs. Dawa, and I exchanged smiles as Tenzin cleared his throat and began. "Okay, so today I'm going to show you some of the math I've been working on this term. I'll start with a unit I feel confident about—fractions—and then I'll talk about something I'm still improving on."

He flipped to his first page. "This is my work on adding and subtracting fractions. At first, I didn't really understand why we had to find common denominators, but then I worked through this problem where I had to add two-thirds and five-sixths. Once I visualized the fractions using a diagram, it clicked. See here?" He pointed to a neatly drawn model. "This helped me realize how common denominators make the fractions 'speak the same language.'"

Mrs. Dawa nodded, visibly impressed. "That's really clear, Tenzin. I didn't learn it that way when I was in school!"

Encouraged, Tenzin flipped to another page. "Now, here's where I struggle—solving word problems with fractions. This one asked me to figure out how much fabric was left after using one and three-quarters meters out of four meters. I got confused about how to set it up, but then I asked for help, and Ms. Singh showed me how to break it into steps. I made mistakes at first, but here's my final version. I got it!"

"That's a big improvement," I chimed in. "Tenzin also practiced explaining his process out loud to a partner, which really helped him solidify the steps."

Tenzin nodded. "Yeah, and now I feel like I can tackle word problems better. My next goal is to apply these skills when we do our project next week. We're building scale models of dream houses, and I'll need to use fractions for scaling measurements. I'm excited about it!"

His mom clapped her hands together. "I can't wait to see that project. You're doing great!"

As Tenzin wrapped up the conference, I could see how proud he was of his progress. He had clearly connected the work to his goals and was ready for what came next.

Conclusion

We all know that the art of teaching is incredibly complex. Teaching would be easy if every student in our class enjoyed the topics we were trying to teach. We all know "those" kids. They're the kids who love learning, who always try hard, and who are engaged in what you're teaching no matter what you do. But this isn't the reality of our classrooms. We teach in complex classrooms with diverse learners, who are beautifully complicated.

When students are given authentic opportunities to share their ideas and experiences, they become active participants in their learning. Voice and choice supports meaningful connections to content, especially for diverse learners, including those who are neurodiverse or multilingual, or who have experienced trauma. Voice and choice works in all classrooms but, most importantly, it also works in complex classrooms.

Offering even small, visible choices that honor who our students are fosters autonomy, which leads to greater confidence, motivation, and ownership over learning.

Creating a classroom that values voice and choice involves risk and discomfort for both teachers and students. It requires transparency, reflection, and a willingness to shift traditional roles. But when it is done intentionally, grounded in pedagogy and a clear understanding of curriculum and child development, it becomes a powerful pathway to deeper learning and greater educational equity.

The beauty of voice and choice is that it moves the needle closer to that ideal. When students are able to bring themselves into the topics, projects, and tasks they complete at school, their level of enjoyment and engagement creeps up. In our experience, when we offer our students the ability to make their learning what they need it to be, they become "those" kids who love learning, try hard, and are engaged in what they're learning.

We want to end by using one of the strategies we shared in this book, sticky note feedback. Here are your next steps:

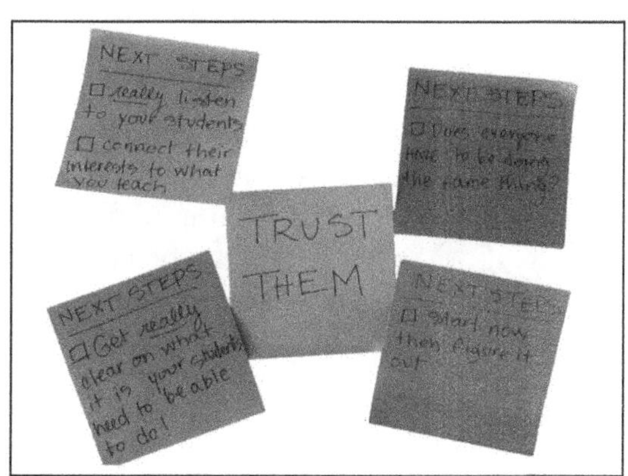

Acknowledgments

This book was born from a chance encounter with Pembroke's Mary Macchiusi at the National Council of Teachers of English Conference in Anaheim in 2022. We are grateful that Mary saw the spark of something in a short presentation we gave about how we centred voice and choice in our English language arts classroom and approached us with a fateful question: "Have you ever thought about writing a book?" We want to also thank our editor, David Kilgour, for helping us shape our words into the book you are now reading.

We were invited to that conference by Angela Stockman, who has long supported our work and elevated our voices. We want to thank Angela for inspiring us in this journey, inviting us to contribute to some of her projects, and encouraging us at every step. Other authors have also supported our work through the years. We would like to thank Derrique DeGagne, who invited us to contribute to a book called *Weaving Hope through Alberta's Education System*, in which we wrote a literacy manifesto. The act of writing this helped us to really articulate what mattered to us most. Heather Lyon also invited us to contribute to her book, *Engagement Is Not a Unicorn (It's a Narwhal)*. Erin would also like to thank Dr. Robert Kelly, whose work in creativity in education underlies all this work.

Because we are full-time educators with busy lives, the process of writing this book has been a long one. We want to thank the colleagues who have supported us through their encouragement, kindness, and laughter. These are the people who know we always take the work seriously and remind us to never take ourselves seriously. Thank you to all the educators who have attended our workshops, built on our ideas, and brought this work to their classrooms. Thank you to Natasha Ruzycki, Ryan Molyneux, Ian Fero, Jennifer Batycky, Alison Moller, and Paige Applehof for always saying, "Yes, and..."

We want to thank our families for being patient with us as we have worked through weekends and late nights. Thank you for feeding us, caffeinating us, and reminding us that this work matters. Erin thanks her sister, Selby, and her parents, Kevin and Dale. Tara thanks her husband, Mark, kids Grayson, Layla, and Scarlett, and her parents, Helen and Victor (who passed away while we were writing).

This may sound kind of nuts, but we also want to thank each other. What luck it was that we ended up teaching together at the same school. It is a rare and beautiful thing to find a colleague who makes you a better teacher every day. It is even rarer when that person becomes a friend who makes you a better human. We don't think either of us would have guessed then that we would be here now, years later, as lifelong friends.

References

Amos, M. (2022, September 26). Building student leadership skills through participation in parent-teacher conferences. *Edutopia*. Retrieved from https://www.edutopia.org/article/student-led-parent-teacher-conferences

Atwell, N. (2007). *Lessons that change writers*. Heinemann.

Berger, R. (2014, March). When students lead their learning. *Educational Leadership, 71*(6). Retrieved from https://www.ascd.org/el/articles/when-students-lead-their-learning

Bicard, D. F., Ervin, A., Bicard, S. C., & Baylot-Casey, L. (2012). Differential effects of seating arrangements on disruptive behavior of fifth-grade students during independent seatwork. *Journal of Applied Behavior Analysis, 45*(2), 407–411. https://doi.org/10.1901/jaba.2012.45-407

Brenner, C. A. (2022). Self-regulated learning, self-determination theory and teacher candidates' development of competency-based teaching practices. *Smart Learning Environments, 9*(3). https://doi.org/10.1186/s40561-021-00184-5

Canadian Heritage (Ed.). (n.d.). Historical thinking concepts. *Historical Thinking Concepts | Historical Thinking Project*. Retrieved from https://historicalthinking.ca/historical-thinking-concepts

Cass, M., & Sanderson, O. (2019, May). To transform your industry, look at someone else's. *IDEO*. Retrieved from https://www.ideo.com/journal/to-transform-your-industry-look-at-someone-elses

Cone, T., Annaisie, T., & Goel, A. (n.d.). *Stoke Deck*. Retrieved from https://stokedeck.io/

Csikszentmihalyi, M. (1996). *Creativity: Flow and the psychology of discovery and invention*. HarperCollins.

Dam, R. F., & Siang, T. Y. (2024, July 6). Affinity diagrams: How to cluster your ideas and reveal insights. *The Interaction Design Foundation*. Retrieved from https://www.interaction-design.org/literature/article/affinity-diagrams-learn-how-to-cluster-and-bundle-ideas-and-facts

Development Impact and You. (n.d.). Development impact and you. Retrieved from https://diy-toolkit.org/

Dweck, C. S. (2016). *Mindset: The new psychology of success*. Ballantine Books.

Edutopia [@edutopia]. (2023, February 11). *From @counseloradventures: Ready to spread some kindness! The 3rd and 4th graders had a lot of fun decorating sleeves for our local coffee shop. We talked about spreading kindness in our community and we can't wait to deliver the sleeves*. Instagram. Retrieved from https://www.instagram.com/edutopia/p/Cohxp0MshgZ/

Edutopia. (2010, July 2). Pixar's Randy Nelson on the collaborative age. *YouTube*. https://www.youtube.com/watch?v=QhXJe8ANws8&t=1s

Elmansy, R. (2024, April 15). Design thinking tools: Reverse brainstorming. Retrieved from *Designorate:* https://www.designorate.com/design-thinking-tools-reverse-brainstorming/

Emergent Futures Lab. (n.d.). Definition of enabling constraint. Retrieved from https://emergentfutureslab.com/innovation-glossary/enabling-constraint

Falchikov, N. (2004). Involving students in assessment. *Psychology Learning and Teaching, 3*(2), 102–108. https://doi.org/10.2304/plat.2003.3.2.102

Felsman, P., Gunawardena, S., & Seifert, C. M. (2020). Improv experience promotes divergent thinking, uncertainty tolerance, and affective well-being. *Thinking Skills and Creativity, 35*, 100632. Retrieved from https://doi.org/10.1016/j.tsc.2020.100632

Felsman, P., Seifert, C. M., & Himle, J. A. (2019). The use of improvisational theater training to reduce social anxiety in adolescents. *The Arts in Psychotherapy, 63*, 111–117. Retrieved from https://doi.org/10.1016/j.aip.2018.12.001

Gielen, S., Peeters, E., Dochy, F., Onghena, P., & Struyven, K. (2010). Improving the effectiveness of peer feedback for learning. *Learning and Instruction, 20*(4), 304–315. https://doi.org/10.1016/j.learninstruc.2009.08.007

Hattie, J., & Timperley, H. (2007). The power of feedback. *Review of Educational Research, 77*(1), 81–112. https://doi.org/10.3102/003465430298487

Hennigan, L., & Botteroff, C. (2024, July 25). What is a Kanban board? The ultimate guide. Retrieved from *Forbes:* https://www.forbes.com/advisor/business/software/what-is-kanban-board/

Herring, O. (n.d.). *TASK Party*. Retrieved from https://oliverherringstudio.com/section/363344-TASK.html

Idea Generator. (n.d.). Unlimited free ideas generated by AI. Retrieved from https://www.getvoila.ai/ai-tools/idea-generator

IDEO. (2014). *Design thinking for libraries: A toolkit for patron-centered design.* Retrieved from https://www.ideo.com/journal/design-thinking-for-libraries

IDEO. (2015). *The field guide to human-centered design.* Retrieved from http://www.designkit.org

Institute of Play at the Connected Learning Alliance. (2024, April 11). *Connected Learning Alliance.* Retrieved from https://clalliance.org/institute-of-play/

Iyengar, S. S., & Lepper, M. R. (2000). When choice is demotivating: Can one desire too much of a good thing? *Journal of Personality and Social Psychology, 79*(6), 995–1006. https://doi.org/10.1037/0022-3514.79.6.995

Johnstone, K. (n.d.). *Keith Johnstone.* Retrieved from https://www.keithjohnstone.com/

Kelly, R. W. (2016). *Creative development: Transforming education through design thinking, innovation, and invention.* Brush Education Inc.

Kelly, R. W. (2020). *Collaborative creativity: Educating for creative development, innovation, and entrepreneurship.* Brush Education Inc.

Khan Academy. (n.d.). Free online courses, lessons & practice. *Khan Academy.* Retrieved from https://www.khanacademy.org/

Kittle, P. (n.d.). Workshop handouts. *Penny Kittle Website.* Retrieved from https://www.pennykittle.net/workshop-hand

Kleon, A. (2012). *Steal like an artist: 10 things nobody told you about being creative.* Workman Publishing Company.

Little, A. W. (Nancy), & Allan, J. (1980). Student-led parent-teacher conferences. *The Reading Teacher, 34*(3), 280–285. Retrieved from https://www.jstor.org/stable/42868875

Malaguzzi, L. (n.d.). 100 languages. Retrieved from *Reggio Children:* https://www.reggiochildren.it/en/reggio-emilia-approach/100-linguaggi-en/

Marzano, R. J., Marzano, J. S., & Pickering, D. J. (2003). *Classroom management that works: Research-based strategies for every teacher.* Association for Supervision and Curriculum Development.

Miller, M. (2024, September 17). *Ditch that textbook.* Retrieved from https://ditchthattextbook.com/

National Council of Teachers of Mathematics. (n.d.). Mathematical proficiency: The five strands.

Nauss, S. A. (2010). Student-led conferences: Students taking responsibility. *ERIC.* Retrieved from https://files.eric.ed.gov/fulltext/ED516784.pdf

Nicolson, S. (1971). How not to cheat children: The theory of loose parts. *Landscape Architecture, 62,* 30–34.

O'Dell, R. (n.d.). Mini moves for writers. *YouTube.* Retrieved from https://www.youtube.com/@minimovesforwriters4503

Pezzetti, K. (2018). Daily oral language, the bell tolls for thee: A critique of daily sentence-editing exercises. *Language Arts Journal of Michigan, 34*(1). https://doi.org/10.9707/2168-149X.2182

Reggio Emilia Approach. (n.d.). *Reggio Children.* Retrieved from https://www.reggiochildren.it/en/reggio-emilia-approach/

Ripp, P. (2017). *Passionate readers.* Taylor & Francis.

Ryan, R. M., & Deci, E. L. (2000). Self-determination theory and the facilitation of intrinsic motivation, social development, and well-being. *American Psychologist, 55*(1), 68–78. Retrieved from https://selfdeterminationtheory.org/SDT/documents/2000_RyanDeci_SDT.pdf

Scott, D., & Lock, J. (Eds.). (2022). *Teacher as designer: Design thinking for educational change.* Springer Singapore.

Şişman, C., & Bahadır, E. (2021). The effects of student-led conferences on the improvement of 21st-century career and life skills. *International Journal of Learning, Teaching and Educational Research, 20*(4), 152–169. https://doi.org/10.26803/ijlter.20.4.8

Stockman, A. (2016). *Make writing: 5 teaching strategies that turn writer's workshop into a maker space.* Times 10 Publications.

Stockman, A. (2023). *The writing workshop teacher's guide to multimodal composition (K–5).* Routledge.

Tolentino, B. (n.d.). Tolentino teaching (Resources for English teachers). *YouTube.* Retrieved from https://www.youtube.com/channel/UCxVnC3TU90xGfwGGJj--dHA

Topping, K. J. (1998). Peer assessment between students in colleges and universities. *Review of Educational Research, 68*(3), 249–276. Retrieved from https://www.jstor.org/stable/1170598

Ültanır, E. (2012, July). An epistemological glance at the constructivist approach: Constructivist learning in Dewey, Piaget, and Montessori. *International Journal of Instruction, 5*(2), 195–212.

UNICEF (Ed.). (2021, June 1). Importance of transferable skills development in Latin America and the Caribbean. *UNICEF.* Retrieved from https://www.unicef.org/lac/en/reports/importance-transferable-skills-development-latin-america-and-caribbean van Gennip, N. A. E., Segers, M. S. R., & Tillema, H. H. (2010). Peer assessment as a collaborative learning activity: The role of interpersonal variables and conceptions. *Learning and Instruction, 20*(4), 280–290. https://doi.org/10.1016/j.learninstruc.2009.08.010

Vygotsky, L. S. (1978). *Mind in society: The development of higher psychological processes* (M. Cole, V. John-Steiner, S. Scribner, & E. Souberman, Eds.). Harvard University Press. Retrieved from https://doi.org/10.2307/j.ctvjf9vz4

Index